THE ALKAINE HEALTHY MEN

100+ Recipes to Understand pH, Eat Well, and Reclaim Your Health! Plant-Based Recipes Are Included! Boost your Weight-Loss!

By

Laura Green

TABLE OF CONTENT

Each specific diet plan for health is created to produce somewhat similar results, but each follows a different path to achieve those goals. Experts developed the Alkaline Diet to help our bodies work effectively and efficiently, curbing the threats of many diseases. This is because the human body requires an optimal pH level for all enzymes to function effectively. The neutrality of the internal environment can only be maintained with a good and balanced diet. Since most foods are more acidic, we all suffer from intestinal acidity, indigestion, and other related diseases. The alkaline diet can solve all these problems as it offers a proper approach to maintain the internal pH level.

Let's start with a bit of review of our chemistry lessons and remember what pH is. A simple definition is how much concentration of hydrogen ions there is in our body. The acronym pH is an abbreviation for "hydrogen potency." The "p" stands for "potent" or the German word for power, and "H" stands for the symbol for the element hydrogen. The pH scale ranges from 1 to 14. Seven is neutral. A pH below seven is acidic. Solutions that have a pH above seven are alkaline.

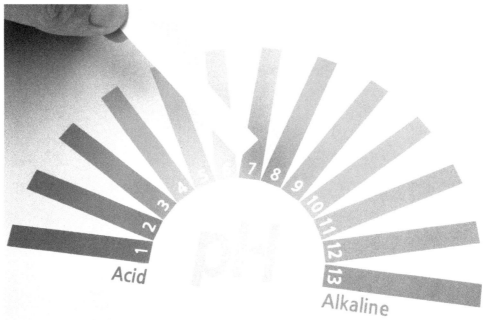

To have good health, our bodies must be somewhat alkaline. The pH of our blood and other cellular fluids should be around a pH between 7.365 and 7.45. It is essential to understand that pH levels vary significantly throughout the body. Some parts will be acidic, while others will be alkaline. There is no set level. For example, our stomach is loaded with hydrochloric acid, giving it a pH of between 2 and 3.5. This makes it very acidic. It needs to be so acidic to break down the foods we consume and kill harmful bacteria. Our saliva has a pH between 6.8 and 7.3. The skin has a pH level of 4 to 6.5. This acts as a protective barrier from the environment. Our urine has a pH that ranges from alkaline to acidic. It all depends on what you eat.

The most critical measure is the pH of your blood. It needs to stay in a very narrow range between 7.365 and 7.45. This may sound simple, but instead of operating on a mathematical scale, our pH operates on a logarithmic scale in multiples of ten. This means that it will take ten times the amount of alkalinity to neutralize an acid. A pH of five will be 100 times more acidic than a pH of seven. A pH of four will be 1,000 times more acidic. Does this help you understand?

Don't start stressing about being in or out of this range. Remember that our bodies are pretty good at regulating the pH of our blood. However, our bodies don't "find" the balance. It has many parts that do, and it keeps the pH of your blood between 7.365 and 7.45 at all times. If you make poor lifestyle and food choices, your body works harder to maintain balance. If you want to address inflammation and acidity in your body by changing your food choices to more alkaline foods, this will help balance your system and return your body to its best vitality.

BLOOD pH

You know that the body is constantly working to maintain healthy pH levels in your body. The tricky thing is that three fluids in the body are typically at slightly different pH levels. But, overall, they are mainly controlled by the same things. So the first thing we're going to look at is the pH of the blood.

The normal pH range for blood is 7.35 to 7.45. This means that the blood usually is alkaline or basic by nature. However, compared to stomach acid, which is between 3 and 5.5, you can see a big difference. The stomach is supposed to be at this acidic level to break down the food you eat. Ironically, if your stomach acid becomes more acidic or more basic, it can create the same symptoms of acid reflux, but that's another matter. This low pH helps you digest your food and destroys germs that may enter your stomach.

What can cause your blood pH to change or reach abnormal levels?

Health problems are usually the most common cause of your blood becoming too alkaline or acidic. In addition, a change in normal blood pH levels can signal a medical emergency or health condition. This may include:

- Poisoning
- Drug overdose
- Bleeding
- Shock
- Infection
- Gout
- Lung disease
- Kidney disease
- Heart disease
- Diabetes
- Asthma

Acidosis refers to when the blood pH level drops below 7.35 and begins to become too acidic. Alkalosis refers to when the pH level of the blood increases to more than 7.45 and starts to become too alkaline. Two main organs work hard to help maintain normal pH levels in the blood:

- Kidneys - These organs work to remove acid through urine to excrete it.
- Lungs - These organs work by getting rid of carbon dioxide through breathing.

The different forms of blood alkalosis and acidosis depend significantly on the cause. However, the two leading causes are:

- Metabolic - These types of problems occur most often when the pH of the blood changes due to a problem with a condition in the kidneys.
- Respiratory - These types of problems occur most often when the blood pH changes due to a respiratory or pulmonary condition.

It is common for blood pH levels to be tested as part of a blood gas test. This type of test is also called an ABG test or arterial blood gas test. It works by measuring how much carbon dioxide and oxygen are in your blood. Your general practitioner may choose to test your blood pH as a regular part of your annual health screenings or if you already have certain health conditions. Blood pH tests require blood to be drawn with a needle. The lab will receive the blood sample and perform the test.

There are at-home blood pH tests that you can do by pricking your finger. These tests will not give you an accurate reading like a test in your doctor's office. Using a urine pH test will not show you the pH level of your blood, but it can let you know if something is wrong.

Let's take a moment to take a closer look at some reasons why your blood pH levels move outside of the normal range.

High blood pH, also known as alkalosis, occurs if the pH of your blood rises above the normal range. There are many reasons for high blood pH levels. For example, you can have a temporary increase in blood pH with simple illnesses. Certain foods can also cause your blood to become more alkaline. However, there are also more serious causes for this alkalosis that can create additional problems.

The first is fluid loss. Losing too much water can cause the pH levels in your blood to rise. This is because you also lose some electrolytes in your blood, minerals, and salts when you lose water. These include potassium and sodium. In addition, diarrhea, vomiting, and sweating can cause excess fluid loss.

Medications and diuretics can also cause a person to urinate more often, leading to increased pH levels in the blood. Treatment for fluid loss requires making sure you are getting plenty of fluids and replacing electrolytes. Some sports drinks can be used for this purpose. Your doctor can also review your medications and stop those that may be causing fluid loss.

Next, kidney problems can cause high pH levels in the blood. The kidneys play an essential role in maintaining normal blood pH. Therefore, a kidney problem can cause a buildup of alkalinity in the blood. This is because the kidneys do not remove excess alkaline substances through the urine. For example, the kidneys may improperly filter bicarbonate in the blood. Medications can regulate it.

When there is acidosis in the blood, it can affect how every organ in your body works. Low blood pH is a more common problem than high blood pH. Acidosis is often a warning sign of some health problem that is not being controlled.

Some health conditions can cause natural acids to build up in the blood. Some forms of acids that can end up lowering the pH of the blood include:

- Carbonic acid
- Hydrochloric acid
- Phosphoric acid
- Sulfuric acid
- Ketogenic acids
- Lactic acid

An improper diet can cause problems. Eating an unbalanced diet can create a temporary low pH level in the blood. Not eating enough or going for long periods without eating can make more acid in the blood. Try to avoid eating too many acid-forming foods, which include:

- Grains - rice, pasta, bread, and flour
- fish
- Meat
- Eggs
- Poultry - turkey and chicken
- Dairy products - yogurt, cheese, and cow's milk

Balance your blood pH by eating more alkaline foods. These more often include dried, frozen, and fresh fruits and fresh and cooked vegetables. Stay away from fad or starvation diets. Instead, when trying to lose weight, do so healthily and safely by following a balanced diet.

Another cause of low blood pH levels is due to diabetic ketoacidosis. If you have diabetes, your blood can end up becoming acidic if you don't regulate your blood sugar levels properly. Diabetic ketoacidosis occurs when your body can't make enough insulin or use it properly.

Insulin helps move sugar from the foods we eat into the cells of the body. This is where the body burns it as fuel. If insulin cannot be used, the body begins to break down the fat stored in the body for fuel. This releases a wasted acid known as ketones. If the body cannot regulate this process, the acid will build up and trigger a low pH in the blood.

You must seek emergency care if your blood sugar level exceeds 300 milligrams per deciliter. If you suffer from any of the following symptoms, talk to your doctor:

- Confusion
- Stomach pain
- Shortness of breath
- Shortness of breath
- Vomiting or nausea
- Weakness or fatigue
- Frequent urination
- Excessive thirst

Diabetic ketoacidosis is most often a sign that diabetes is not being treated properly and is out of control. This can sometimes be the first sign of diabetes for some people. Making sure your diabetes is well treated will help keep your blood pH in balance. It may require a strict diet and exercise plan, insulin injections, and medications to stay healthy.

The third cause of low blood pH is metabolic acidosis. This is when low blood pH is caused by kidney disease or failure. This occurs when the kidneys fail in removing acids from the body through urination. This will increase the acids in your body and lower your blood pH.

The most common symptoms of metabolic acidosis include.

- Heavy breathing
- Fast heartbeat
- Headaches
- Vomiting and nausea
- Loss of appetite
- Weakness and fatigue

Treatment for this problem often includes medications to help the kidneys work better, but a kidney transplant or dialysis is the only solution for severe cases. Dialysis works by cleansing the blood.

The final cause of low pH in the blood is respiratory acidosis. When the lungs are probably not working to remove carbon dioxide from the body quickly, blood pH levels drop. This will happen more often if a person has a chronic or severe lung condition, such as:

- Diaphragm disorders
- Chronic obstructive pulmonary disease
- Pneumonia
- Bronchitis

- Sleep apnea
- Asthma

People who are obese, have had surgery, or abuse opioid painkillers or sedatives are at increased risk of developing respiratory acidosis. In some cases, the kidneys can take over the situation and remove excess blood acids through excretion. As a result, a person may need to receive extra oxygen and medications such as steroids and bronchodilators to help the lungs function correctly. In very severe cases, mechanical ventilation and intubation may be needed in individuals with respiratory acidosis to bring the blood pH back to normal.

- Urine pH

The next type of pH we will examine is urine pH. Urine is composed of waste products, salts, and water that are excreted through the kidneys. The balance of these different compounds can affect the acidity level of the urine.

According to the American Association for Clinical Chemistry, the average urine pH is 6.0, but it can range from 4.5 to 8.0. Any level below 5.0 is considered acidic urine, and any level above 8.0 is considered basic urine.

Sometimes different labs have different ranges on what they consider normal pH levels for urine. One of the main things that affect the pH of your urine is the things you eat. If you go to your doctor, he or she will often ask you what foods you ate before evaluating the results of a urine pH test.

If, before a test, you ate more acidic foods, your urine will be more acidic. The same is true if you have eaten more alkaline foods. If a person has extremely high pH levels in their urine, meaning it is more alkaline, it could be the result of problems, such as:

- Urinary tract infections
- Kidney stones
- Other kidney-related disorders

A person may also have high pH levels in their urine if they have had prolonged vomiting. This is because vomiting causes the body to get rid of stomach acid, which causes body fluids to become more essential.

When urine is acidic, it creates an environment conducive to kidney stones. When urine is acidic, it can also be a sign of several severe medical conditions, such as:

- Hunger
- Diarrhea
- Diabetic ketoacidosis

As you will notice, much of this is the same as blood pH levels. Certain medications can affect the pH of the urine. Sometimes doctors will ask a patient to discontinue certain medications the day or night before doing a urinalysis.

- Saliva pH

The last pH we will look at is the pH of saliva. The usual range of saliva pH is from 6.2 to 7.6. The things you drink and eat can change the pH of your saliva.

Just like any other area of your body, your mouth needs to maintain a balanced pH. Saliva pH levels can drop below 5.5 when you've had a lot of acidic drinks. When this happens, the acids in your mouth begin to break down the enamel on your teeth.

If your tooth enamel becomes too thin, the dentin will be exposed. This can end up causing discomfort when you consume sugary, cold, or hot drinks. Just to give you an example of foods and drinks that can do this, here are some numbers:

- Cherries have a pH of 4
- American cheese has a pH of 5
- White wine has a pH of 4
- Soft drinks have a pH of 3

It's easy to spot unbalanced pH levels in your saliva. Some of the most common indicators are:
- Tooth decay
- Sensitivity to cold or hot drinks or foods
- Persistent bad breath

If you want, you can also test the pH of your saliva. Your saliva's pH can be tested: you will need to find pH strips. Once you have your strips, this is what you need to do:
- Make sure you don't eat or drink anything for at least two hours before the test.
- Let your mouth fill with saliva and then swallow or spit it out.
- Let your mouth fill with saliva again, and then place a small amount on one of your pH strips.
- The strip will then react to your saliva. It will change color based on how alkaline or acidic your saliva is. The container the pH strips came with should show a color chart. Put your strip next to the chart to match the colors and determine the pH level of your saliva.

To make sure the pH of your saliva stays balanced, you must eat foods that are in a healthy pH range. It's also important that you don't deprive yourself of important vitamins and minerals. There are a few more effective ways to make sure the pH of your saliva stays balanced.
- Stay away from sugary drinks. If you must drink them, try to drink them quickly and chase them with water. Sipping sugary beverages for an extended period of time does more damage.
- Limit black coffee. Adding a little cream, unsweetened, can help reduce the acidity of coffee.
- Avoid brushing your teeth immediately after consuming high-acid beverages such as beer, wine, cider, juice, or soda. These types of beverages soften tooth enamel. If you brush your teeth too soon after consuming these things, you will further damage your enamel.
- Chew sugar-free gum after consuming any beverage or food. Chewing gum will cause your mouth to produce more saliva and help bring your pH level back to normal. It is also believed that xylitol can prevent bacteria from sticking to your tooth enamel.
- Keep yourself hydrated, so be sure to drink plenty of water.

1) Chocolate quinoa porridge

Preparation time: 15 minutes   **Cooking time:** 30 minutes   **Portions: 4**

Ingredients:

- ✓ 1 cup uncooked quinoa, rinsed and drained
- ✓ 1 cup unsweetened almond milk
- ✓ 1 cup unsweetened coconut milk
- ✓ Pinch of sea salt

Directions:

- ❖ Heat a small non-stick frying pan over medium heat and cook the quinoa for about 3 minutes or until lightly toasted, stirring often.
- ❖ Add the almond milk, coconut milk and a pinch of salt and stir to combine.
- ❖ Increase the heat to high and bring to the boil.

Ingredients:

- ✓ 2 tablespoons of cocoa powder
- ✓ 2 tablespoons maple syrup
- ✓ ½ teaspoon organic vanilla extract
- ✓ ½ cup fresh strawberries, peeled and sliced

- ❖ Reduce the heat to low and cook, uncovered for about 20-25 minutes or until all the liquid is absorbed, stirring occasionally.
- ❖ Remove from the heat and immediately stir in the cocoa powder, maple syrup and vanilla extract.
- ❖ Serve immediately with a garnish of strawberry slices.

2) Buckwheat porridge with walnuts

Preparation time: 15 minutes   **Cooking time:** 7 minutes   **Portions: 2**

Ingredients:

- ✓ ½ cup buckwheat
- ✓ 1 cup of alkaline water
- ✓ 2 tablespoons of chia seeds
- ✓ 15-20 almonds
- ✓ 1 cup unsweetened almond milk

Directions:

- ❖ In a large bowl, soak the buckwheat groats in water overnight.
- ❖ In 2 other bowls, soak the chia seeds and almonds respectively.
- ❖ Drain the buckwheat and rinse well.
- ❖ In a non-stick pan, add the buckwheat and almond milk over medium heat and cook for about 7 minutes or until creamy.

Ingredients:

- ✓ ½ teaspoon cinnamon powder
- ✓ 1 teaspoon organic vanilla extract
- ✓ 3-4 drops of liquid stevia
- ✓ ¼ cup of fresh mixed berries

- ❖ Drain the chia seeds and almonds well.
- ❖ Remove the pan from the heat and stir in the almonds, chia seeds, cinnamon, vanilla extract and stevia.
- ❖ Serve hot with a berry garnish.

3) Fruity oatmeal

Preparation time: 15 minutes   **Cooking time:** 10 minutes   **Portions: 4**

Ingredients:

- ✓ 4 cups of alkaline water
- ✓ 1 cup steel-cut dry oats
- ✓ 1 large banana, peeled and mashed

Directions:

- ❖ In a large pan, add the water and oats over medium-high heat and bring to the boil.
- ❖ Reduce the heat to low and simmer for about 20 minutes, stirring occasionally.

Ingredients:

- ✓ 1½ cups of fresh mixed berries (your choice)
- ✓ ¼ cup walnuts, finely chopped

- ❖ Remove from the heat and cool slightly.
- ❖ Add the mashed banana and stir to combine.
- ❖ Cover with strawberries and walnuts and serve.

4) Baked walnut oatmeal

Preparation time: 15 minutes   **Cooking time:** 45 minutes   **Portions: 5**

Ingredients:

- ✓ 1 tablespoon linseed meal
- ✓ 3 tablespoons of alkaline water
- ✓ 3 cups unsweetened almond milk
- ✓ ¼ cup maple syrup
- ✓ 2 tablespoons coconut oil, melted and cooled
- ✓ 2 teaspoons of organic vanilla extract

Directions:

- ❖ Lightly grease an 8x8-inch baking dish. Set aside.
- ❖ In a large bowl, add the flaxseed meal and water and beat until well combined. Set aside for about 5 minutes.
- ❖ In the bowl of the flax mixture, add the remaining ingredients except the oats and nuts and mix until well combined.
- ❖ Add the oats and nuts and stir gently to combine.
- ❖ Place the mixture in the prepared baking tin and spread it out in an even layer.

Ingredients:

- ✓ 1 teaspoon cinnamon powder
- ✓ 1 teaspoon organic baking powder
- ✓ ¼ teaspoon of sea salt
- ✓ 2 cups old rolled oats
- ✓ ½ cup almonds, chopped
- ✓ ½ cup walnuts, chopped
- ❖ Cover the baking tray with plastic wrap and refrigerate for about 8 hours.
- ❖ Preheat the oven to 350 degrees F. Place a wire rack in the centre of the oven.
- ❖ Remove the tray from the refrigerator and let it rest at room temperature for 15-20 minutes.
- ❖ Remove the plastic film and mix the oatmeal mixture well.
- ❖ Bake for about 45 minutes.
- ❖ Remove from the oven and set aside to cool slightly.
- ❖ Serve hot.

5) Almond fritters

Preparation time: **Cooking time:**   **Portions: 4**

Ingredients:

- ✓ Coconut oil, 3 tablespoons
- ✓ Almond milk, 1 c.
- ✓ Baking powder, 1 teaspoon

Directions:

- ❖ Place each of the dry fixings in a dish and whisk to mix.
- ❖ Add two tablespoons of coconut oil together with the almond milk to the dry elements and mix well until everything is combined.
- ❖ Place a frying pan over medium heat and put a teaspoon of coconut to melt. Swirl it around in the pan to coat it.

Ingredients:

- ✓ Arrowroot powder, 2 tablespoons
- ✓ Almond flour, 1 c.

- ❖ Pour a ladleful of batter into the pan and use the bottom of the ladle to smooth out the pancake.
- ❖ Bake for three minutes until the edges are bubbly and brown.
- ❖ Flip the pancake over and cook for a further three minutes until cooked through.
- ❖ Continue to cook the pancakes until all the batter has been used.

6) Amaranth porridge

Preparation time: **Cooking time:**   **Portions: 2**

Ingredients:
- ✓ Cinnamon, 1 tablespoon
- ✓ Coconut oil, 2 tablespoons
- ✓ Amaranth, 1 c.

Ingredients:
- ✓ Alkaline water, 2 c.
- ✓ Almond milk, 2 c.

Directions:
- ❖ Put the water and milk in a saucepan. Set to medium-hot and let it boil.

- ❖ Add the amaranth and lower the heat to low. Stew for half an hour, stirring occasionally.
- ❖ Remove from the heat, add the copra oil and cinnamon, mix well, serve hot.

7) Banana porridge

Preparation time: **Cooking time:**   **Portions: 2**

Ingredients:
- ✓ Ground almonds, .25 c.
- ✓ Liquid stevia, 3 drops
- ✓ Barley, .5 c.

Ingredients:
- ✓ Sliced banana, 1
- ✓ Unsweetened almond milk, 1 c.

Directions:
- ❖ Mix stevia, 1/2 cup almond milk and barley in a bowl.
- ❖ Refrigerate, covered for six hours.

- ❖ Remove from the fridge and mix with the remaining milk. Pour into a saucepan and place on medium. Allow the mixture to cook for five minutes.

8) Courgette muffins

Preparation time: **Cooking time:**   **Portions: 16**

Ingredients:
- ✓ Halls
- ✓ Cinnamon, 1 teaspoon
- ✓ Baking powder, 1 tablespoon
- ✓ Almond flour, 2 c.
- ✓ Vanilla extract, 1 teaspoon
- ✓ Almond milk, .5 c.
- ✓ Grated courgettes, 2

Ingredients:
- ✓ Overripe bananas, 3
- ✓ Almond butter, .25 c.
- ✓ Alkaline water, 3 tablespoons
- ✓ Ground linseed, 1 tablespoon
- ✓ Optional ingredients:
- ✓ Chopped walnuts, .25 c.
- ✓ Chocolate chips, .25 c.
- ❖ Mash the bananas in a saucepan and put all the leftover contents in. Stir well.
- ❖ Spread the concoction evenly in a cupcake tin.
- ❖ Bake for 25 minutes.

Directions:
- ❖ You need to heat your cooking appliance to 375 degrees. Spray a cupcake pan with cooking spray.
- ❖ Place the water and linseed in a bowl.

9) Tofu stew with vegetables

Preparation time: **Cooking time:**   **Portions: 4**

Ingredients:
- ✓ Halls
- ✓ Chopped basil, 2 tablespoons
- ✓ Chopped hard-boiled tofu, 3 c.
- ✓ Diced peppers (red, bell), 2 pieces.
- ✓ Olive oil, 1 tablespoon

Ingredients:
- ✓ Turmeric
- ✓ Chopped cherry tomatoes, 2 c.
- ✓ Chopped onions, 2
- ✓ Cayenne

Directions:
- ❖ Place a greased frying pan over medium heat and heat the pan.
- ❖ Put the peppers together with the onions, prepare for five minutes.

- ❖ Add the tofu, cayenne, salt and turmeric. Cook for a further eight minutes.
- ❖ Garnish with basil.

10) Courgette fritters

Preparation time: **Cooking time:**   **Portions: 8**

Ingredients:
- ✓ Shallots, finely chopped, .5 c.
- ✓ Finely chopped jalapeno, 2
- ✓ Olive oil, 2 tablespoons
- ✓ Ground linseed, 4 tablespoons

Ingredients:
- ✓ Halls
- ✓ Grated courgettes, 6
- ✓ Alkaline water, 12 tablespoons

Directions:
- ❖ Place the flaxseed and water in a bowl and mix well. Set aside.
- ❖ Place a large frying pan over medium heat and heat the oil. Add the pepper, salt and courgettes. Cook for three minutes and place the courgettes in a bowl.

- ❖ Add the linseed mixture and the shallots and mix well.
- ❖ Heat up a griddle that has been sprayed with cooking spray. Pour a few courgettes onto the preheated griddle and cook for three minutes per side until golden brown.
- ❖ Repeat until the mixture is completely exhausted.

11) Quinoa with pumpkin

Preparation time: **Cooking time:**   **Portions: 2**

Ingredients:
- ✓ Chia seeds, 2 teaspoons
- ✓ Pumpkin pie spice, 1 teaspoon
- ✓ Pumpkin puree, .25 c.

Ingredients:
- ✓ Crushed banana, 1
- ✓ Unsweetened almond milk, 1 c.
- ✓ Cooked quinoa, 1 c.
- ❖ Refrigerate overnight.
- ❖ When ready to eat, take it out of the fridge and enjoy.

Directions:
- ❖ Put all the ingredients in a container.
- ❖ Make sure the lid is sealed and shake well to combine.

12) Avocado toast

Preparation time: **Cooking time:**   **Portions: 4**

Ingredients:
- ✓ Dulse flakes, sliced radish, sliced red onion, for garnish - optional
- ✓ Sea salt, 0.5 teaspoons
- ✓ Fresh coriander leaves, 1 tablespoon
- ✓ Chopped onion, 1 tablespoon

Ingredients:
- ✓ Garlic, 2 cloves
- ✓ Jalapeno
- ✓ Avocado, 2
- ✓ Sweet potato, unpeeled, cut into 4 thick slices lengthwise
- ❖ While the sweet potato toast is cooking, add the salt, coriander, onion, garlic, jalapeno and avocado to an extremely electric food processor and blend until smooth. Adjust the amount of salt as necessary.
- ❖ Divide the avocado spread over each of the sweet potato toast slices. Top each slice with the desired toppings. Enjoy your meal.

Directions:
- ❖ Place each of the potato slices in a slot of the toaster and toast them for four cycles, or until they are cooked. You can also toast them in the oven if you don't have a regular toaster oven. You want them to be tender enough that you can easily pierce them with a fork. Carefully arrange the cooked toast on plates.

13) Frozen banana breakfast bowl

Preparation time: **Cooking time:**   **Portions: 1**

Ingredients:
- ✓ Chia seeds, hemp seeds, unsweetened coconut flakes, for garnish - optional
- ✓ Pumpkin seed protein powder, 4 tablespoons

Ingredients:
- ✓ Bananas, 2

Directions:
- ❖ Peel and then slice the bananas. Place them thinly in a freezer-safe container and freeze overnight.
- ❖ The next morning, add the bananas to a food processor and blend until a smooth, creamy consistency is achieved, much like that of soft-serve ice cream.

- ❖ Process the pumpkin protein powder through the bananas until it is just combined.
- ❖ Pour into a serving dish and add the desired toppings, if desired, and enjoy.

14) Vegetarian lettuce rolls

Preparation time: 20 minutes   **Cooking time**: 10 minutes   **Portions: 4**

Ingredients:

- ✓ For filling:
- ✓ 1 teaspoon of olive oil
- ✓ 2 cups fresh shiitake mushrooms, chopped
- ✓ 2 teaspoons of tamari, divided
- ✓ 1 cup of cooked quinoa
- ✓ 1 teaspoon fresh lime juice
- ✓ 1 teaspoon organic apple cider vinegar
- ✓ ¼ cup shallots, chopped
- ✓ Sea salt and freshly ground black pepper, to taste
- ✓ For the creamy sauce:
- ✓ 5 ounces of tofu silken, pressed, drained and chopped
- ✓ 1 small clove of garlic, minced

Ingredients:

- ✓ ¼ cup plain almond butter
- ✓ 1 teaspoon fresh lime juice
- ✓ Sea salt and freshly ground black pepper, to taste
- ✓ For enclosures:
- ✓ 8 medium-sized lettuce leaves
- ✓ ¼ cup cucumber, peeled and julienned
- ✓ ¼ cup of carrot, peeled and julienned
- ✓ ¼ cup of cabbage, shredded

Directions:

- ❖ For the filling, in a frying pan, heat the oil over medium heat and cook the mushrooms and 1 teaspoon of tamari for about 5-8 minutes, stirring often.
- ❖ Stir in the quinoa, lime juice, vinegar and remaining tamari and cook for about 1 minute, stirring constantly.
- ❖ Add the shallot, salt and black pepper and immediately remove from the heat.

- ❖ Set aside to cool.
- ❖ Meanwhile, for the sauce: in a food processor, add all the ingredients and pulse until a smooth sauce is obtained.
- ❖ Arrange the lettuce leaves on serving plates.
- ❖ Place the quinoa filling evenly on each leaf and cover with cucumbers, carrots and cabbage.
- ❖ Serve alongside the creamy sauce.

15) Oatmeal, tofu and spinach burger

Preparation time: 15 minutes   **Cooking time:** 16 minutes   **Portions: 4**

Ingredients:

- ✓ 1 pound firm tofu, drained, pressed and crumbled
- ✓ ¾ cup rolled oats
- ✓ ¼ cup of linseed
- ✓ 2 cups of frozen, thawed, squeezed and chopped cabbage
- ✓ 1 medium onion, finely chopped
- ✓ 4 cloves of garlic, minced

Directions:

- ❖ In a large bowl, add all the ingredients except the oil and the green salads and mix until well combined.
- ❖ Set aside for about 10 minutes.
- ❖ Cut the dough into meatballs of the desired size.

Ingredients:

- ✓ 1 teaspoon ground cumin
- ✓ 1 teaspoon red pepper flakes, crushed
- ✓ Sea salt and freshly ground black pepper, to taste
- ✓ 2 tablespoons of olive oil
- ✓ 6 cups of fresh salad

- ❖ In a non-stick frying pan, heat the oil over medium heat and cook the meatballs for 6-8 minutes per side.
- ❖ Serve these meatballs alongside green salad.

16) Hamburger with beans, nuts and vegetables

Preparation time: 20 minutes   **Cooking time**: 25 minutes   **Portions**: 4

Ingredients:

- ✓ ½ cup walnuts
- ✓ 1 carrot, peeled and chopped
- ✓ 1 celery stalk, chopped
- ✓ 4 shallots, chopped
- ✓ 5 cloves of garlic, minced
- ✓ 2¼ cups canned black beans, rinsed and drained

Directions:

- ❖ Preheat the oven to 400 degrees F. Line a baking tray with baking paper.
- ❖ In a food processor, add the walnuts and pulse until finely ground.
- ❖ Add the carrot, celery, shallot and garlic and chop finely.
- ❖ Transfer the vegetable mixture into a large bowl.
- ❖ In the same food processor, add the beans and give a pulse until they are chopped.
- ❖ Add 1 1/2 cups of sweet potatoes and pulse to form a chunky mixture.

Ingredients:

- ✓ 2½ cups sweet potato, peeled and grated
- ✓ ½ teaspoon red pepper flakes, crushed
- ✓ ¼ teaspoon cayenne pepper
- ✓ Sea salt and freshly ground black pepper, to taste
- ✓ 12 cups of fresh vegetables

- ❖ Transfer the bean mixture to the bowl with the vegetable mixture.
- ❖ Stir in the remaining sweet potato, spices, salt and black pepper and mix until well combined.
- ❖ Make 8 equal-sized patties from the bean mixture.
- ❖ Arrange the meatballs on the prepared baking tray in a single layer.
- ❖ Bake for about 25 minutes.
- ❖ Divide the vegetables between the serving plates and top each with 2 meatballs.
- ❖ Serve immediately.

17) Avocado stuffed with tofu and broccoli

Preparation time: 20 minutes   **Cooking time**: 15 minutes   **Portions**: 6

Ingredients:

For the marinade:
- ✓ ¼ cup fresh parsley leaves, chopped
- ✓ 1 small clove of garlic, minced
- ✓ 1 teaspoon fresh lemon peel, finely grated
- ✓ 1 tablespoon Dijon mustard
- ✓ ¼ cup of olive oil
- ✓ 2 tablespoons fresh lemon juice
- ✓ ¼ teaspoon of ground cumin
- ✓ Sea salt and freshly ground black pepper, to taste

Directions:

- ❖ For the marinade: in a large bowl, add all the ingredients except the tofu and beat until well combined.
- ❖ Add the tofu and broccoli and cover generously with the marinade.
- ❖ Cover the bowl and refrigerate for about 1 hour.
- ❖ Preheat the grill to medium-high heat. Generously grease the grill grate.
- ❖ Place the tofu slices on the grill and cook for about 2 minutes per side.
- ❖ Grill the broccoli florets for about 8-10 minutes, turning occasionally.

Ingredients:

- ✓ 1 (8-ounce) package of solid tofu, drained, pressed and cut into ½ inch slices
- ✓ 1 cup of broccoli florets
  For the stuffed avocados:
- ✓ 1 tablespoon fresh chives, chopped
- ✓ 3 firm avocados, peeled, halved and pitted
- ✓ Sea salt and freshly ground black pepper, to taste
- ✓ 2 tablespoons fresh parsley, chopped

- ❖ Remove the tofu and broccoli from the grill and transfer to a large bowl.
- ❖ Set aside to cool slightly.
- ❖ Then, cut the tofu and broccoli into small pieces.
- ❖ Transfer the tofu and broccoli to a bowl with the chives and mix well.
- ❖ Sprinkle the avocado halves with salt and black pepper.
- ❖ Stuff each half evenly with the tofu mixture.
- ❖ Garnish with parsley and serve immediately.

18) Brussels sprouts with walnuts

Preparation time: 15 minutes   **Cooking time:** 15 minutes   **Portions: 2**

Ingredients:
- ✓ ½ pound Brussels sprouts, cut and halved
- ✓ 1 tablespoon olive oil
- ✓ 2 cloves of garlic, minced
- ✓ ½ teaspoon red pepper flakes, crushed

Directions:
- ❖ In a large pot of boiling water, place a steamer basket.
- ❖ Place the asparagus in the basket of the steamer and steam, covered, for about 6-8 minutes.
- ❖ Drain the asparagus well.

Ingredients:
- ✓ Sea salt and freshly ground black pepper, to taste
- ✓ 1 tablespoon fresh lemon juice
- ✓ 1 tablespoon pine nuts

- ❖ In a large frying pan, heat the oil over medium heat and fry the garlic and red pepper flakes for about 30-40 seconds.
- ❖ Add the Brussels sprouts, salt and black pepper and fry for about 4-5 minutes.
- ❖ Add the lemon juice and fry for about 1 minute more.
- ❖ Add the pine nuts and remove from the heat.
- ❖ Serve hot.

19) Broccoli with cabbage

Preparation time: 20 minutes   **Cooking time:** 1 hour 20 minutes   **Portions: 8**

Ingredients:
- ✓ 3 tablespoons of coconut oil, divided by
- ✓ ¼ small yellow onion, chopped
- ✓ 1 teaspoon chopped garlic
- ✓ 1 teaspoon fresh ginger root, peeled and chopped
- ✓ 1 cup of broccoli florets

Directions:
- ❖ In a large frying pan, melt 2 tablespoons of coconut oil over medium-high heat and fry the onion for about 3-4 minutes.
- ❖ Add the garlic and ginger and fry for about 1 minute.
- ❖ Add the broccoli and stir to combine well.
- ❖ Immediately, reduce the heat to medium-low and cook for about 2-3 minutes, stirring constantly.

Ingredients:
- ✓ 2 cups fresh cabbage, hard ribs removed and chopped
- ✓ ½ cup of coconut cream
- ✓ ¼ teaspoon red pepper flakes, crushed
- ✓ 1 teaspoon fresh parsley, finely chopped

- ❖ Add the cabbage and cook for about 3 minutes, stirring often.
- ❖ Add the coconut cream and the remaining coconut oil and mix until smooth.
- ❖ Add the red pepper flakes and simmer for about 5-10 minutes, stirring occasionally or until the curry has the desired thickness.
- ❖ Remove from the heat and serve hot with a garnish of parsley.

20) Mushrooms with parsley

Preparation time: 15 minutes   **Cooking time:** 15 minutes   **Portions: 2**

Ingredients:
- ✓ 2 tablespoons of olive oil
- ✓ 2-3 tablespoons of chopped onion
- ✓ ½ teaspoon chopped garlic

Directions:
- ❖ In a frying pan, heat the oil over medium heat and fry the onion and garlic for 2-3 minutes.

Ingredients:
- ✓ 12 ounces of sliced fresh mushrooms
- ✓ 1 tablespoon fresh parsley, chopped
- ✓ Sea salt and freshly ground black pepper, to taste

- ❖ Add the mushrooms and cook for 8-10 minutes or until cooked through, stirring frequently.
- ❖ Add the parsley, salt and black pepper and remove from the heat.
- ❖ Serve hot.

21) Garlic broccoli

Preparation time: 15 minutes   **Cooking time:** 8 minutes   **Portions: 3**

Ingredients:

- ✓ 1 tablespoon olive oil
- ✓ 2 cloves of garlic, minced
- ✓ 2 cups of broccoli florets

Ingredients:

- ✓ 2 tablespoons of alkaline water
- ✓ Sea salt and freshly ground black pepper, to taste

Directions:

- ❖ In a large frying pan, heat the oil over medium heat and fry the garlic for about 1 minute.
- ❖ Add the broccoli and fry for about 2 minutes.

- ❖ In a large frying pan, heat the oil over medium heat and fry the garlic for about 1 minute.
- ❖ Add the broccoli and fry for about 2 minutes.

22) Broccoli with peppers

Preparation time: 15 minutes   **Cooking time:** 10 minutes   **Portions: 5**

Ingredients:

- ✓ 2 tablespoons of olive oil
- ✓ 4 cloves of garlic, minced
- ✓ 1 large white onion, sliced
- ✓ 2 cups of small broccoli florets

Directions:

- ❖ In a large frying pan, heat the oil over medium heat and fry the garlic for about 1 minute.

Ingredients:

- ✓ 3 red peppers, seeded and sliced
- ✓ ¼ cup of homemade vegetable stock
- ✓ Sea salt and freshly ground black pepper, to taste

- ❖ Add the onion, broccoli and peppers and fry for about 5 minutes.
- ❖ Add the stock and fry for about 4 minutes more.
- ❖ Serve hot.

23) Spicy okra

Preparation time: 15 minutes   **Cooking time:** 13 minutes   **Portions: 2**

Ingredients:

- ✓ 1 tablespoon olive oil
- ✓ ½ teaspoon of caraway seeds
- ✓ ¾ pound okra pods, trimmed and cut into 2-inch pieces

Directions:

- ❖ In a large frying pan, heat the oil over medium heat and fry the cumin seeds for 30 seconds.
- ❖ Add the okra and fry for 1-1½ minutes.
- ❖ Reduce the heat to low and cook, covered, for 6-8 minutes, stirring occasionally.

Ingredients:

- ✓ ½ teaspoon of red chilli powder
- ✓ 1 teaspoon ground coriander
- ✓ Sea salt and freshly ground black pepper, to taste
- ❖ Uncover and increase heat to medium.
- ❖ Add the chilli powder and cilantro and cook for a further 2-3 minutes.
- ❖ Season with salt and remove from the heat.
- ❖ Serve hot.

24) Spicy cauliflower

Preparation time: 15 minutes   **Cooking time:** 20 minutes   **Portions: 4**

Ingredients:
- ✓ ¼ cup alkaline water
- ✓ 2 medium fresh tomatoes, chopped
- ✓ 2 tablespoons of extra virgin olive oil
- ✓ 1 small white onion, chopped
- ✓ ½ tablespoon fresh ginger root, peeled and chopped
- ✓ 3 medium garlic cloves, chopped
- ✓ 1 jalapeño pepper, seeded and chopped
- ✓ 1 teaspoon ground cumin

Directions:
- ❖ In a blender, add ¼ cup water and the tomatoes and pulse until pureed. Set aside.
- ❖ In a large frying pan, heat the oil over medium heat and fry the onion for about 4-5 minutes.
- ❖ Add the ginger, garlic, jalapeño pepper and spices and fry for about 1 minute.

Ingredients:
- ✓ 1 teaspoon ground coriander
- ✓ 1 teaspoon cayenne pepper
- ✓ ¼ teaspoon ground turmeric
- ✓ 3 cups cauliflower, chopped
- ✓ Sea salt and freshly ground black pepper, to taste
- ✓ ½ cup of warm alkaline water
- ✓ ¼ cup fresh parsley leaves, chopped

- ❖ Add the tomato puree and cauliflower and cook for about 3-4 minutes, stirring constantly.
- ❖ Add the hot water and bring to the boil.
- ❖ Reduce the heat to medium-low and simmer, covered, for about 8-10 minutes or until the desired doneness of the cauliflower.
- ❖ Remove from the heat and serve hot with a garnish of parsley.

25) Aubergine curry

Preparation time: 15 minutes   **Cooking time:** 35 minutes   **Portions: 3**

Ingredients:
- ✓ 1 tablespoon of coconut oil
- ✓ 1 medium onion, finely chopped
- ✓ 2 cloves of garlic, minced
- ✓ ½ tablespoon fresh ginger root, peeled and chopped
- ✓ 1 Serrano pepper, seeded and chopped

Directions:
- ❖ In a large frying pan, melt the coconut oil over medium heat and fry the onion for 8-9 minutes.
- ❖ Add the garlic, serrano pepper and salt and fry for 1 minute.
- ❖ Add the tomato and cook for 3-4 minutes, crushing with the back of a spoon.

Ingredients:
- ✓ Sea salt and freshly ground black pepper, to taste
- ✓ 1 medium tomato, finely chopped
- ✓ 1 large aubergine, diced
- ✓ 1 cup unsweetened coconut milk
- ✓ 2 tablespoons fresh parsley, chopped
- ❖ Add the aubergines and salt and cook for 1 minute, stirring occasionally.
- ❖ Stir in the coconut milk and bring to a gentle boil.
- ❖ Reduce the heat to medium-low and simmer, covered for 15-20 minutes or until completely done.
- ❖ Remove from the heat and serve with a garnish of parsley.

26) Lemon cabbage with shallots

Preparation time: 15 minutes   **Cooking time:** 20 minutes   **Portions: 4**

Ingredients:
- ✓ 1 tablespoon extra virgin olive oil
- ✓ 1 lemon, seeded and thinly sliced
- ✓ 1 white onion, thinly sliced
- ✓ 3 cloves of garlic, minced

Directions:
- ❖ In a large frying pan, heat the oil over medium heat and cook the lemon slices for 5 minutes.
- ❖ Using a slotted spoon, remove the lemon slices from the pan and set aside.

Ingredients:
- ✓ 2 lbs. fresh cabbage, hard ribs removed and chopped
- ✓ ½ cup shallots, chopped
- ✓ Sea salt and freshly ground black pepper, to taste

- ❖ In the same pan, add the onion and garlic and fry for about 5 minutes.
- ❖ Add the cabbage, shallots, salt and pepper and cook for 8-10 minutes.
- ❖ Add the lemon slices and stir until well combined.
- ❖ Remove from the heat and serve hot.

27) Vegetables with apple

Preparation time: 15 minutes   **Cooking time:** 16 minutes   **Portions: 4**

Ingredients:

For the sauce:
- ✓ 3 small garlic cloves, chopped
- ✓ 1 teaspoon fresh ginger root, peeled and chopped
- ✓ 1 tablespoon fresh orange peel, finely grated
- ✓ ½ cup of fresh orange juice
- ✓ 1 tablespoon maple syrup
- ✓ 2 tablespoons of tamari
- ✓ 2 tablespoons organic apple cider vinegar

Directions:

- ❖ For the sauce: in a large bowl, add all the ingredients and with a wire whisk, beat until well combined. Set aside.
- ❖ In a large frying pan, heat the oil over medium-high heat and fry the carrot and broccoli for about 4-5 minutes.

Ingredients:

For vegetables and apple:
- ✓ 1 tablespoon olive oil
- ✓ 2 cups of carrots, peeled and cut into julienne strips
- ✓ 1 head of broccoli, cut into florets
- ✓ 1 cup red onion, chopped
- ✓ 2 apples, core and slices

- ❖ Add the onion and fry for about 4-5 minutes.
- ❖ Add the sauce and cook for about 2-3 minutes, stirring frequently.
- ❖ Stir in the apple slices and cook for about 2-3 minutes.
- ❖ Remove from the heat and serve hot.

28) Cabbage with apple

Preparation time: 15 minutes   **Cooking time:** 12 minutes   **Portions: 4**

Ingredients:

- ✓ 2 teaspoons of coconut oil
- ✓ 1 large apple, cored and thinly sliced
- ✓ 1 onion, thinly sliced
- ✓ 1 ½ pounds of cabbage, finely chopped

Directions:

- ❖ In a non-stick pan, melt 1 teaspoon of coconut oil over medium heat and fry the apple for about 2-3 minutes.
- ❖ Transfer the apple to a bowl.
- ❖ In the same pan, melt 1 teaspoon of coconut oil over medium heat and fry the onion for about 2-3 minutes.

Ingredients:

- ✓ 1 tablespoon fresh thyme, chopped
- ✓ 1 fresh red chilli pepper, chopped
- ✓ 1 tablespoon organic apple cider vinegar

- ❖ Add the cabbage and fry for about 4-5 minutes.
- ❖ Add the cooked apple slices, thyme and vinegar and cook, covered, for about 1 minute.
- ❖ Remove from the heat and serve hot.

29) Asparagus with herbs

Preparation time: 15 minutes   **Cooking time:** 10 minutes   **Portions: 4**

Ingredients:

- ✓ 2 tablespoons of olive oil
- ✓ 2 tablespoons fresh lemon juice
- ✓ 1 tablespoon organic apple cider vinegar
- ✓ 1 teaspoon chopped garlic

Directions:

- ❖ Preheat the oven to 400 degrees F. Lightly grease a rimmed baking sheet.
- ❖ In a bowl, add the oil, lemon juice, vinegar, garlic, herbs, salt and black pepper and whisk until well combined.

Ingredients:

- ✓ 1 tablespoon fresh parsley, chopped
- ✓ 1 teaspoon dried oregano
- ✓ Sea salt and freshly ground black pepper, to taste
- ✓ 1 lb. fresh asparagus, without ends
- ❖ Arrange the asparagus on the prepared baking tray in a single layer.
- ❖ Cover with half of the herb mixture and stir to coat.
- ❖ Roast for about 8-10 minutes.
- ❖ Remove from the oven and transfer the asparagus to a serving dish.
- ❖ Sprinkle with the remaining herb mixture and serve immediately.

30) Vegetarian Kabobs

Preparation time: 20 minutes   **Cooking time**: 10 minutes   **Portions: 4**

Ingredients:

For the marinade:
- ✓ 2 cloves of garlic, minced
- ✓ 2 teaspoons fresh basil, chopped
- ✓ 2 teaspoons fresh oregano, chopped
- ✓ ½ teaspoon of cayenne pepper
- ✓ Sea salt and freshly ground black pepper, to taste
- ✓ 2 tablespoons fresh lemon juice
- ✓ 2 tablespoons of olive oil

Directions:

- ❖ For the marinade: in a large bowl, add all the ingredients and mix until well combined.
- ❖ Add the vegetables and toss to coat them well.
- ❖ Cover the bowl and place in the fridge to marinate for at least 6-8 hours.
- ❖ Preheat the grill to medium-high heat. Generously grease the grill grate.

Ingredients:

For the vegetables:
- ✓ 16 large button mushrooms, quartered
- ✓ 1 yellow pepper, seeded and diced
- ✓ 1 red pepper, seeded and diced
- ✓ 1 orange pepper, seeded and diced
- ✓ 1 green pepper, seeded and diced

- ❖ Remove the vegetables from the bowl and thread onto pre-soaked wooden skewers.
- ❖ Place the skewers on the grill and cook for about 8-10 minutes or until cooked through, turning occasionally.
- ❖ Remove from the grill and serve hot.

31) Tofu with Brussels sprouts

Preparation time: 15 minutes   **Cooking time:** 15 minutes   **Portions: 4**

Ingredients:

- ✓ 1 tablespoon olive oil, separated
- ✓ 8 ounces of extra-fine tofu, drained, pressed and sliced
- ✓ 2 cloves of garlic, minced
- ✓ 1/3 cup pecans, toasted and chopped

Directions:

- ❖ In a frying pan, heat ½ tablespoon of oil over medium heat and fry the tofu for about 6-7 minutes or until golden brown.
- ❖ Add the garlic and pecans and fry for about 1 minute.
- ❖ Add the apple sauce and cook for about 2 minutes.
- ❖ Add the parsley and remove from the heat.

Ingredients:

- ✓ 1 tablespoon unsweetened apple juice
- ✓ ¼ cup fresh parsley, chopped
- ✓ ½ pound Brussels sprouts, trimmed and cut into wide strips

- ❖ With a slotted spoon, transfer the tofu to a plate and set aside.
- ❖ In the same pan, heat the remaining oil over medium-high heat and cook the Brussels sprouts for about 5 minutes.
- ❖ Stir in the cooked tofu and remove from the heat.
- ❖ Serve immediately.

32) Tofu with broccoli

Preparation time: 15 minutes   **Cooking time:** 13 minutes   **Portions: 3**

Ingredients:

- ✓ 1 (12-ounce) package of solid tofu, drained, pressed and cut into 5 slices
- ✓ 2 tablespoons of coconut oil, divided by
- ✓ 2 cups of small broccoli florets

Directions:

- ❖ In a large non-stick frying pan, melt 1 tablespoon of coconut oil over medium-high heat and cook the tofu for 4-5 minutes per side or until crispy.
- ❖ Using a slotted spoon, place the tofu slices on a paper towel-lined plate to absorb the extra oil.
- ❖ Then, cut each slice of tofu into equal-sized pieces.
- ❖ Meanwhile, in a large microwaveable bowl, add the broccoli florets and water.

Ingredients:

- ✓ ¼ cup alkaline water
- ✓ ½ tablespoon chopped garlic
- ✓ ½ tablespoon fresh ginger root, chopped
- ✓ Sea salt and freshly ground black pepper, to taste
- ❖ Cover the bowl and microwave on High for about 5 minutes.
- ❖ Remove from the microwave and drain the broccoli.
- ❖ In the same pan, melt the remaining coconut oil over medium heat and fry the garlic and ginger for about 1 minute.
- ❖ Add the tofu, broccoli and black pepper and cook for 2 minutes, tossing occasionally.
- ❖ Remove from the heat and serve hot.

33) Tempeh in tomato sauce

Preparation time: 20 minutes   **Cooking time:** 1 hour 20 minutes   **Portions:** 4

Ingredients:

- ✓ ½ cup of extra virgin olive oil, divided by
- ✓ 2 packets of tempeh (8 oz), cut into half-inch horizontal slices
- ✓ 1 large yellow onion, chopped
- ✓ 3 cloves of garlic, minced
- ✓ 1 teaspoon dried oregano, crushed
- ✓ 1 teaspoon dried thyme, crushed
- ✓ ½ teaspoon of red chilli powder

Directions:

- ❖ Preheat the oven to 350 degrees F.
- ❖ In a large bowl, add 2 tablespoons of oil and the tempeh slices and stir to coat well.
- ❖ In a large frying pan, heat ¼ cup of oil over medium-high heat and cook the tempeh slices for about 5-7 minutes.
- ❖ Carefully switch sides and cook for about 5-7 minutes.
- ❖ Transfer the cooked tempeh slices to a plate lined with paper towels.
- ❖ Set aside to drain.
- ❖ Meanwhile, in another non-stick pan, heat the remaining oil over medium-low heat and fry the onion, garlic, herbs and spices for about 8-10 minutes.

Ingredients:

- ✓ ½ teaspoon red pepper flakes, crushed
- ✓ 1 large green pepper, seeded and thinly sliced
- ✓ 1 large yellow pepper, seeded and thinly sliced
- ✓ 2 cups fresh tomatoes, finely chopped
- ✓ ¼ cup of homemade tomato paste
- ✓ 1 teaspoon organic apple cider vinegar
- ✓ 1 tablespoon maple syrup
- ❖ Add the peppers and fry for about 4-5 minutes, stirring occasionally.
- ❖ Add the remaining ingredients and mix until well combined.
- ❖ Remove from heat.
- ❖ In the bottom of a large casserole dish, arrange the tempeh slices.
- ❖ Spread the tomato mixture evenly over the tempeh slices.
- ❖ Cover the casserole dish well with a piece of foil.
- ❖ Bake for about 1 hour.
- ❖ Remove from the oven and set aside to cool slightly.
- ❖ Serve hot.

34) South West Stuffed Sweet Potatoes

Preparation time: 30 minutes   **Cooking time:** 30 minutes   **Portions:** 2

Ingredients:

- ✓ 2 sweet potatoes
- ✓ 2 tablespoons of coconut oil
- ✓ ½ cup of black beans, rinsed and drained
- ✓ 1 shallot, sliced
- ✓ 3 cups of spinach
- ✓ A pinch of dried red pepper
- ✓ Pinch of cumin
- ✓ 1 avocado, peeled and sliced

Directions:

- ❖ Preheat the oven to 400°F/205°C. Clean the sweet potatoes and pierce them several times with a fork. Place the sweet potatoes on a baking sheet lined with baking paper and bake about 50 minutes or until soft.
- ❖ Leave the sweet potatoes to cool for 5 minutes.
- ❖ While the sweet potatoes are cooling, heat the frying pan over a medium heat and add the coconut oil, shallots and black beans.

Ingredients:

Condiment
- ✓ 3 tablespoons of olive oil
- ✓ 1 lime, squeezed
- ✓ 1 teaspoon of cumin
- ✓ Handful of coriander, chopped
- ✓ Salt and pepper

- ❖ Cook for 5 minutes then add the spinach, dried chilli flakes and cumin. Cook for another 1 minute.
- ❖ In a small bowl, whisk together the dressing ingredients.
- ❖ Slice the sweet potatoes in the centre and stuff them with the black bean mixture. Cover with slices of avocado.
- ❖ Pour the dressing over the sweet potatoes and serve.

35) Coconut cauliflower with herbs and spices

Preparation time: 30 minutes   **Cooking time:**   **Portions:** 2

Ingredients:

- ✓ ¼ cup of coconut oil, melted
- ✓ ½ tablespoon ground cumin
- ✓ ¼ teaspoon of ground coriander
- ✓ 1 teaspoon ground turmeric
- ✓ ¼ teaspoon black pepper, ground
- ✓ 1 large cauliflower, cut into small florets

Directions:

- ❖ Preheat oven to 425°F/220°C. In a large bowl, mix together coconut oil, cumin, coriander, turmeric and black pepper. Add the cauliflower and stir until well coated.

Ingredients:

- ✓ 2 tablespoons of toasted pine nuts
- ✓ 1 tablespoon coriander, chopped
- ✓ ½ tablespoon mint, coarsely chopped
- ✓ 1 tablespoon of sultanas
- ✓ Himalayan salt

- ❖ Spread the cauliflower on the baking tray and place in the oven for 20 minutes. Remove from the oven and transfer to a serving bowl.
- ❖ Mix the pine nuts, coriander, mint, sultanas and salt with the cauliflower and serve hot.

36) Quinoa and Brussels sprouts salad

Preparation time: 5 minutes   **Cooking time:** 0 minutes   **Portions: 2**

Ingredients:
- ¼ cup quinoa, cooked
- ½ pound (227 g) Brussels sprouts, halved, diced, roasted
- 2 tablespoons dried blueberries
- 1 medium white onion, peeled, sliced and caramelised

Directions:
- ❖ Take a small bowl, pour in the orange juice and lime juice, add the orange zest and then stir until combined.

Ingredients:
- ⅓ teaspoon of salt
- ⅛ teaspoon of cayenne pepper
- ½ orange, squeezed
- ½ teaspoon of orange peel
- 1 tablespoon lime juice
- ❖ Take a salad bowl, put the remaining ingredients in, drizzle with the orange juice mixture and then toss until mixed.
- ❖ Serve immediately.

37) Mango and jicama salad

Preparation time: 5 minutes   **Cooking time:** 15 minutes   **Portions: 1**

Ingredients:
- 1 mango, peeled and cut into pieces
- 1 cup of sliced jicama
- 1 cup of sliced pepper

Directions:
- ❖ In a small bowl, combine the mango, pepper and jicama.

Ingredients:
- Juice of 1 lime
- 1 tablespoon chilli powder
- ❖ Squeeze the lime juice over the vegetables. Sprinkle with chilli powder.
- ❖ Refrigerate for 15 minutes to allow the flavours to meld and enjoy.

38) Asparagus and roasted mushroom salad

Preparation time: 10 minutes   **Cooking time:** 15 minutes   **Portions: 2**

Ingredients:
- ½ bunch of asparagus, blunted
- 1 pint of cherry tomatoes
- ½ cup mushrooms, halved
- 1 carrot, peeled and cut into small pieces

Directions:
- ❖ Preheat oven to 425ºF (220ºC).
- ❖ In a bowl, add the asparagus, tomatoes, mushrooms, carrot and pepper. Add the coconut oil, garlic powder and salt. Stir to coat the vegetables evenly.

Ingredients:
- 1 red or yellow pepper, seeded and cut into small pieces
- 1 tablespoon of coconut oil
- 1 tablespoon garlic powder
- 1 teaspoon sea salt
- ❖ Transfer the vegetables to a baking tray, place in the preheated oven and roast for 15 minutes, or until the vegetables are tender.
- ❖ Transfer the vegetables to a large bowl. Refrigerate, if desired.
- ❖ Divide the vegetables between two bowls and serve hot or cold.

39) Thai green salad

Preparation time: 10 minutes   **Cooking time:** 0 minutes   **Portions: 2**

Ingredients:
- 4 cups chopped iceberg lettuce
- 1 cup of bean sprouts
- 2 carrots, cut into thin slices or spirals
- 1 courgette, cut into thin strips or spirals
- 1 shallot, finely chopped
- 2 tablespoons chopped almonds

Directions:
- ❖ In a large bowl, combine the lettuce, bean sprouts, carrots, courgettes, shallots and almonds.

Ingredients:
- Juice of 1 lime
- 1 garlic clove
- 1 teaspoon tamarind paste
- 1 packet of stevia
- ½ teaspoon of sea salt
- ❖ In the small bowl of a food processor, add the lime juice, garlic, tamarind, stevia and salt. Blend to combine.
- ❖ Pour the dressing over the vegetables and mix well.
- ❖ Divide evenly between two bowls and serve.

40) Avocado and quinoa salad

Preparation time: 10 minutes   **Cooking time**: 0 minutes   **Portions**: 2

Ingredients:
- ✓ 1 cup of cooked and cooled quinoa
- ✓ 1 avocado, diced
- ✓ 1 cup cherry tomatoes, halved
- ✓ 1 cup cucumber, peeled and diced
- ✓ ¼ cup chopped coriander

Ingredients:
- ✓ 1 tablespoon garlic powder
- ✓ 1 tablespoon onion powder
- ✓ 1 teaspoon sea salt
- ✓ 1 tablespoon freshly squeezed lemon juice

Directions:
- ❖ In a large bowl, mix together the quinoa, avocado, tomatoes, cucumber, cilantro, garlic powder, onion powder, salt and lemon juice.

- ❖ Chill for 15 minutes to allow the flavours to meld.
- ❖ Serve immediately or store in the fridge for 2 to 3 days.

41) Caprese salad

Preparation time: 5 minutes   **Cooking time**: 0 minutes   **Portions**: 2

Ingredients:
- ✓ 2 large heirloom tomatoes, sliced
- ✓ 1 avocado, sliced

Ingredients:
- ✓ 1 bunch of basil leaves
- ✓ 1 teaspoon sea salt

Directions:
- ❖ n a serving dish, place 1 tomato slice, 1 avocado slice and 1 basil leaf.

- ❖ Repeat the pattern with all the remaining tomato slices, avocado slices and basil leaves.
- ❖ Salt and serve.

42) Tagliatelle with pumpkin and broccoli salad

Preparation time: 10 minutes   **Cooking time**: 50 minutes   **Portions**: 4

Ingredients:
- ✓ 1 spaghetti squash
- ✓ 2 tablespoons of coconut oil
- ✓ 2 cups of cooked broccoli florets
- ✓ 1 red pepper, seedless and cut into strips
- ✓ 1 shallot, chopped

Ingredients:
- ✓ 1 tablespoon sesame oil
- ✓ 1 teaspoon of red pepper flakes
- ✓ 2 teaspoons of sea salt, divided
- ✓ 2 tablespoons of toasted sesame seeds

Directions:
- ❖ Preheat the oven to 350°F (180°C).
- ❖ To roast a pumpkin, cut it in half lengthways and scrape out the seeds. Brush each half with coconut oil and season with 1 teaspoon of sea salt. Place the pumpkin halves with the cut side up on a baking tray and roast in the preheated oven for about 50 minutes, or until tender to the fork.

- ❖ Prepare the pumpkin noodles by removing the inside of the roasted pumpkin with a fork in a large bowl.
- ❖ Add the broccoli, red pepper and shallot.
- ❖ In a small bowl, combine the sesame oil, red pepper flakes and remaining salt. Pour over the vegetables. Stir gently to combine.
- ❖ Garnish with sesame seeds and serve.

43) Broccoli and mandarin salad

Preparation time: 5 minutes   **Cooking time**: 0 minutes   **Portions**: 4

Ingredients:
- ✓ 4 cups of cooked and cooled broccoli florets
- ✓ 2 mandarins without seeds, peeled and separated
- ✓ ⅓ cup of freshly squeezed orange juice
- ✓ 2 tablespoons of sesame oil

Ingredients:
- ✓ 2 cloves of garlic, minced
- ✓ ½ teaspoon of sea salt
- ✓ ¼ teaspoon red pepper flakes

Directions:
- ❖ In a large bowl, combine the broccoli and tangerine sections.
- ❖ In a blender, combine the orange juice, sesame oil, garlic, salt and red pepper flakes. Blend until smooth.

- ❖ Pour the dressing over the broccoli salad. Refrigerate for 1 hour to blend the flavours.
- ❖ Serve cold.

44) Spinach and mushroom salad

Preparation time: 2 minutes   **Cooking time:** 5 minutes   **Portions: 2**

Ingredients:
- ✓ 1 (6-ounce / 170-g) packet of baby spinach leaves
- ✓ ½ cup of roasted and ground almonds
- ✓ 1 tablespoon sesame oil
- ✓ 1 tablespoon apple cider vinegar

Directions:
- ❖ In a large bowl, combine the spinach and almonds.
- ❖ In a small saucepan over low heat, combine the sesame oil, cider vinegar, salt and mushrooms.

Ingredients:
- ✓ 1 teaspoon sea salt
- ✓ 1 cup chopped shiitake mushrooms
- ✓ Water, as required

- ❖ Cook for about 5 minutes, or until the mushrooms are softened, adding water if necessary.
- ❖ Pour the mushroom dressing over the spinach. Stir well to coat the spinach leaves.
- ❖ Serve immediately.

45) Broccoli, asparagus and quinoa salad

Preparation time: 5 minutes   **Cooking time:** 0 minutes   **Portions: 4**

Ingredients:
- ✓ 1 cup of cooked broccoli florets, coarsely chopped
- ✓ 1 cup asparagus, cut and cooked, coarsely chopped
- ✓ 2 cups of cooked and cooled quinoa
- ✓ ½ cup of water

Directions:
- ❖ In a large bowl, combine the broccoli and asparagus.
- ❖ Stir in the quinoa.
- ❖ In a blender, combine the water, lemon juice, coconut oil and salt.
- ❖ Blend until the ingredients are emulsified.

Ingredients:
- ✓ 2 tablespoons freshly squeezed lemon juice
- ✓ 2 tablespoons of coconut oil
- ✓ ½ teaspoon of sea salt

- ❖ Pour the dressing over the salad. Stir to combine.
- ❖ Refrigerate the salad for 15 minutes to chill.
- ❖ Serve cold.

46) Root salad

Preparation time: 15 minutes   **Cooking time:** 0 minutes   **Portions: 2**

Ingredients:
- ✓ 1 red beet, peeled and chopped
- ✓ 1 golden beetroot, peeled and chopped
- ✓ 2 carrots, peeled and cut into pieces

Directions:
- ❖ In a medium bowl, mix together the red beetroot, golden beetroot, carrots, hazelnuts, sultanas and salt.

Ingredients:
- ✓ 2 tablespoons hazelnuts
- ✓ 2 tablespoons of sultanas
- ✓ ½ teaspoon of sea salt
- ❖ Refrigerate for 15 minutes to blend the flavours. Serve.

47) Lush summer salad

Preparation time: 5 minutes   **Cooking time:** 0 minutes   **Portions: 4**

Ingredients:
- ✓ 4 cups chopped iceberg or romaine lettuce
- ✓ 2 cups cherry tomatoes, halved
- ✓ 1 (14.5-ounce / 411-g) can of whole green beans, drained
- ✓ ½ cup of shredded carrot

Directions:
- ❖ In a large bowl, combine the lettuce, tomatoes, green beans, carrot, shallot, cucumber and radishes.

Ingredients:
- ✓ 1 shallot, sliced
- ✓ 1 cucumber, peeled and sliced
- ✓ 2 radishes, thinly sliced

- ❖ Mix well with 2 tablespoons of the seasoning of your choice and serve immediately.

48) Salad of sea vegetables and algae

Preparation time: 5 minutes   **Cooking time:** 0 minutes   **Portions: 2**

Ingredients:

- ✓ 1 cup of dried sea vegetables
- ✓ 1 ounce (28 g) of dried seaweed
- ✓ 1 teaspoon spirulina

Directions:

- ❖ Reconstitute the sea vegetables and dried seaweed according to the package directions.
- ❖ Meanwhile, in a small bowl, mix together the spirulina, cider vinegar and stevia.

Ingredients:

- ✓ 1 teaspoon apple cider vinegar
- ✓ 1 packet of stevia
- ✓ 1 teaspoon of sesame seeds
- ❖ Drain the sea vegetables and seaweed. Squeeze out excess moisture and place in a medium bowl. Add the spirulina mixture and mix.
- ❖ Refrigerate for 1 hour to blend the flavours.
- ❖ Add sesame seeds and serve.

49) Rainbow salad

Preparation time: 10 minutes   **Cooking time:** 0 minutes   **Portions: 2**

Ingredients:

- ✓ 1 mango, peeled, boned and diced
- ✓ ¼ onion, chopped
- ✓ ½ cup cherry tomatoes, halved
- ✓ ½ cucumber, seedless, sliced

Directions:

- ❖ Take a medium bowl, place the mango pieces in it, add the onion, tomatoes, cucumber and pepper and then drizzle with lime juice.

Ingredients:

- ✓ ½ of a green pepper, seedless, sliced
- ✓ ⅓ teaspoon of salt
- ✓ ¼ teaspoon cayenne pepper
- ✓ ¼ key lime, squeezed
- ❖ Season with salt and cayenne pepper, mix until combined, and leave the salad in the fridge for a minimum of 20 minutes.
- ❖ Serve immediately.

50) Rocket salad with basil

Preparation time: 5 minutes   **Cooking time:** 10 minutes   **Portions: 2**

Ingredients:

- ✓ 4 ounces (113 g) arugula
- ✓ ½ cup cherry tomatoes, halved
- ✓ ¼ cup of basil leaves
- ✓ ½ key lime, squeezed

Directions:

- ❖ Prepare the dressing and for this, take a small bowl, put the lime juice in it, add the tahini butter, salt and cayenne pepper and then whisk until combined.

Ingredients:

- ✓ 2 tablespoons of walnuts
- ✓ ¼ teaspoon of salt
- ✓ ⅛ teaspoon of cayenne pepper
- ✓ ½ tablespoon of tahini butter
- ❖ Take a medium bowl, put the rocket, tomatoes and basil leaves in it, pour in the dressing and then massage with your hands.
- ❖ Let the salad stand for 20 minutes, then taste to adjust the dressing and serve.

51) Green cucumber and rocket salad

Preparation time: 5 minutes   **Cooking time:** 0 minutes   **Portions: 2**

Ingredients:

- ✓ ½ cucumber, seedless
- ✓ 4 ounces (113 g) arugula
- ✓ ⅛ teaspoon of salt

Directions:

- ❖ Slice the cucumber, add it to a salad bowl and then add the rocket.

Ingredients:

- ✓ 1 tablespoon lime juice
- ✓ 1 tablespoon olive oil
- ✓ ⅛ teaspoon of cayenne pepper
- ❖ Mix together the lime juice and oil until combined, pour over the salad and then season with salt and cayenne pepper.
- ❖ Stir until combined and then serve.

52) Strawberry and dandelion salad

Preparation time: 10 minutes   **Cooking time:** 7 minutes   **Portions: 2**

Ingredients:
- ✓   ½ onion, peeled, sliced
- ✓   5 strawberries, sliced
- ✓   2 cups dandelion tops, rinsed

Directions:
- ❖   Take a medium frying pan, place it over medium heat, add the oil and let it heat until hot.
- ❖   Add the onion, season with ⅛ teaspoon salt, stir until combined, and then cook for 3 to 5 minutes until tender and golden.
- ❖   In the meantime, take a small bowl, place the strawberry slices in it, drizzle with ½ tablespoon of lime juice and then toss until coated.

Ingredients:
- ✓   1 tablespoon lime juice
- ✓   1 tablespoon of grape oil
- ✓   ¼ teaspoon of salt

- ❖   When the onions have turned golden, add the remaining lime juice, stir until combined, and then cook for 1 minute.
- ❖   Remove the pan from the heat, transfer the onions to a large salad bowl, add the strawberries with their juice and the dandelion, and then sprinkle with the remaining salt. Stir until combined and then serve.

53) Wakame and pepper salad

Preparation time: 15 minutes   **Cooking time:** 0 minutes   **Portions: 2**

Ingredients:
- ✓   1 cup of wakame stalks
- ✓   ½ tablespoon chopped red pepper
- ✓   ½ teaspoon of onion powder
- ✓   ½ tablespoon lime juice

Directions:
- ❖   Put the wakame stalks in a bowl, cover with water, let them soak for 10 minutes and then drain.
- ❖   Meanwhile, prepare the dressing and for this, take a small bowl, add the lime juice, onion, agave syrup and sesame oil and then whisk until combined.

Ingredients:
- ✓   ½ tablespoon agave syrup
- ✓   ½ tablespoon sesame seeds
- ✓   ½ tablespoon sesame oil

- ❖   Place the drained wakame stalks in a large dish, add the pepper, pour in the seasoning and stir until coated.
- ❖   Sprinkle the salad with sesame seeds and serve.

54) Carrot and potato stew with herbs

Preparation time: 10 minutes   **Cooking time**: 50 minutes   **Portions: 4 people**

Ingredients:

- ✓ 1 tablespoon avocado oil
- ✓ 1 cup onion, diced
- ✓ 2 cloves of garlic, crushed
- ✓ 1 teaspoon sea salt
- ✓ 1 teaspoon freshly ground black pepper
- ✓ 3 cups vegetable stock, more if desired

Directions:

- ❖ In a medium saucepan over medium heat, heat the avocado oil. Add the onion, garlic, salt and pepper, and sauté for 2 to 3 minutes, or until the onion is soft.
- ❖ Add the vegetable stock, water, carrot, potato, celery, oregano and bay leaf and stir. Bring to the boil, reduce the heat to medium-low and cook for 30-45 minutes, or until the potatoes and carrots are tender.

Ingredients:

- ✓ 2 cups of water, plus more if desired
- ✓ 3 cups of sliced carrots
- ✓ 1 large potato, diced
- ✓ 2 stalks of celery, diced
- ✓ 1 teaspoon dried oregano
- ✓ 1 dried bay leaf
- ❖ Adjust the seasonings, if necessary, and add more water or vegetable stock if you prefer a softer consistency, in half-cup increments.
- ❖ Pour into 4 soup bowls and enjoy.

55) Berry and mint soup

Preparation time: 5 minutes   **Cooking time**: 0 minutes   **Portions: 1 to 2**

Ingredients:

- ✓ ¼ cup of unrefined whole cane sugar, such as Sucanat
- ✓ ¼ cup of water, more if desired
- ✓ 1 cup mixed berries (raspberries, blackberries, blueberries)

Directions:

- ❖ In a small saucepan over medium-low heat, heat the sugar and water, stirring constantly for 1 to 2 minutes, until the sugar is dissolved. Cool.
- ❖ In a blender, blend together the cooled sugar water with the berries, water, lemon juice and mint leaves until well combined.

Ingredients:

- ✓ ½ cup of water
- ✓ 1 teaspoon freshly squeezed lemon juice
- ✓ 8 fresh mint leaves
- ❖ Transfer the mixture to the refrigerator and allow it to cool completely, about 20 minutes.
- ❖ Pour into 1 large or 2 small bowls and enjoy.

56) Potato and broccoli soup

Preparation time: 10 minutes   **Cooking time**: 25 minutes   **Servings**: 2 to 1

Ingredients:
- ✓ 1 tablespoon avocado oil
- ✓ ½ cup diced onion
- ✓ 2 cloves of garlic, crushed
- ✓ 3 cups vegetable stock
- ✓ 1 (13.5-ounce / 383-g) can of whole coconut milk

Directions:
- ❖ In a large frying pan over medium-high heat, heat the avocado oil. Add the onion and garlic and fry for 2 to 3 minutes, or until the onions are soft.
- ❖ Add the vegetable stock, coconut milk, potatoes, broccoli, salt and pepper and continue to cook for 18-20 minutes, or until the potatoes are soft. Remove from the heat and cool.

Ingredients:
- ✓ 2 cups potatoes, peeled and diced
- ✓ 3 cups of chopped broccoli florets
- ✓ 1 teaspoon sea salt
- ✓ 1½ teaspoons of freshly ground black pepper

- ❖ In a blender, blend the cooled soup until smooth.
- ❖ Adjust seasonings as necessary. Pour into 2 large or 4 small bowls and enjoy.

57) Lush pepper soup

Preparation time: 5 minutes   **Cooking time**: 10 minutes   **Servings**: 2 to 4

Ingredients:
- ✓ 1 teaspoon avocado oil
- ✓ ¼ cup diced onions
- ✓ 2 cloves of garlic, crushed
- ✓ 2 cups of diced red peppers
- ✓ 2 cups of vegetable stock

Directions:
- ❖ In a frying pan over medium-high heat, add the avocado oil, onions, garlic and red peppers and fry for 2 to 3 minutes, or until the onions are soft; allow to cool.
- ❖ In a blender, blend together the sauté, vegetable stock, jalapeño and salt until well combined and completely liquid; adjust the seasonings according to your preference.

Ingredients:
- ✓ ½ to 1 jalapeño, seeded and diced
- ✓ 1 teaspoon sea salt
- ✓ ½ cup diced red peppers
- ✓ ½ cup of diced yellow peppers

- ❖ Transfer the soup to a medium bowl and toss it with the diced red and yellow peppers.
- ❖ Cover and refrigerate for 20-30 minutes to cool or chill overnight.
- ❖ Pour into 2 large or 4 small bowls and enjoy.

58) Cabbage and yellow onion soup

Preparation time: 10 minutes   **Cooking time**: 20 minutes   **Servings**: 2 to 4

Ingredients:
- ✓ 1 tablespoon avocado oil
- ✓ 2 cups thinly sliced yellow onions (3 medium)
- ✓ 1 teaspoon unrefined whole cane sugar, such as Sucanat
- ✓ 1 cup of vegetable stock
- ✓ 2 cups of water

Directions:
- ❖ In a medium saucepan over medium-high heat, heat the avocado oil. Add the onions and sauté for 3-5 minutes, or until the onions start to get soft.
- ❖ Add the sugar and continue to fry, stirring constantly, for 8-10 minutes, or until the onions are slightly caramelised.

Ingredients:
- ✓ 2 tablespoons of coconut amino acids
- ✓ 2 cloves of garlic, crushed
- ✓ ½ teaspoon dried thyme
- ✓ ½ teaspoon of sea salt
- ✓ 3 cabbage stalks, shredded and cut into ribbons (approx. 2 cups)
- ❖ Add the vegetable stock, water, coconut amino acid, garlic, thyme and salt. Reduce the heat to medium-low and simmer for 5-7 minutes. Adjust seasonings as necessary.
- ❖ Add the cabbage and leave on the heat just long enough for it to wilt.
- ❖ Remove from the heat, pour into 2 large or 4 small bowls and serve.

59) Wild rice, mushroom and leek soup

Preparation time: 10 minutes   **Cooking time**: 55 minutes   **Portions: 1 to 2**

Ingredients:

- ✓ ⅓ cup of wild rice
- ✓ 1 cup of sliced cremini mushrooms
- ✓ ½ cup of sliced leeks, only the white part
- ✓ 3 cups of water

Directions:

- ❖ Prepare the wild rice according to the package instructions.
- ❖ In a medium saucepan over high heat, bring the sliced mushrooms, leeks and water to the boil. Boil for 8-10 minutes, or until the mushrooms are soft.

Ingredients:

- ✓ 2 tablespoons of organic white miso
- ✓ ¼ to ½ teaspoon of freshly ground black pepper
- ✓ Sliced shallots, for garnish

- ❖ Add the cooked wild rice, miso and black pepper. Using the back side of a spoon, mash the miso on the side of the pot to break it up, then stir it in.
- ❖ Remove from the heat. Pour into 1 large or 2 small bowls, garnish with chopped shallots and enjoy.

60) Pear and ginger soup

Preparation time: 10 minutes   **Cooking time**: 15 minutes   **Portions: 1 to 2**

Ingredients:

- ✓ 2 teaspoons of avocado oil
- ✓ ½ cup diced onions
- ✓ 2 cloves of garlic, crushed
- ✓ 1 cup of vegetable stock
- ✓ 2 cups of water
- ✓ ¼ cup of coconut milk (canned)

Directions:

- ❖ In a large frying pan over medium-high heat, heat the avocado oil. Add the onion and garlic and fry for 2 to 3 minutes, or until the onions are soft.
- ❖ Add the vegetable stock, water, coconut milk, pears, ginger and salt and cook over a medium-high heat for 8-10 minutes, or until the pears are soft. Remove from the heat and cool.

Ingredients:

- ✓ 2 pears, peeled and diced
- ✓ 1 inch fresh ginger root, chopped
- ✓ ¼ teaspoon of sea salt
- ✓ Sliced radishes, for garnish (optional)
- ✓ Chopped shallots, for garnish (optional)

- ❖ Transfer the soup to a blender and blend until well combined. Adjust seasonings as necessary.
- ❖ Pour immediately into 1 large or 2 small bowls, garnish with the radishes and shallots (if using), and enjoy, or return the soup to the stove to warm slightly over low heat before serving.

61) Asparagus and artichoke soup

Preparation time: 5 minutes   **Cooking time**: 20 minutes   **Servings: 4 cups**

Ingredients:

- ✓ ½ cup diced onion
- ✓ 1 tablespoon avocado oil
- ✓ 2 cloves of garlic, crushed
- ✓ 1 cup of diced potatoes
- ✓ 8 asparagus stalks, cut into small pieces

Directions:

- ❖ In a medium frying pan, fry the onion, avocado oil and garlic over medium-high heat for 2 to 3 minutes, or until the onion is soft.
- ❖ Transfer the sauté to a medium-sized saucepan and add the potatoes, asparagus, vegetable stock, salt and pepper; cook over medium-high heat for 18 to 20 minutes, or until the potatoes are tender. Add more vegetable stock, if necessary, to keep the liquid level between ½ and 1 inch above the contents of the saucepan. Remove from heat and let cool.

Ingredients:

- ✓ 2 cups of vegetable stock
- ✓ ½ to ¾ teaspoon of sea salt
- ✓ ½ teaspoon ground black pepper
- ✓ 2 cups of almond milk
- ✓ 1 tin of artichoke hearts, cut in half and with stem
- ❖ In a blender, blend the cooled soup mixture, the almond milk and the artichokes until everything is well combined and the soup is smooth. Adjust the seasonings to your liking and add more almond milk or vegetable stock to thin it out, if you prefer.
- ❖ Return the soup to the saucepan and heat slightly over low heat before serving.

62) Carrot and celery soup

Preparation time: 15 minutes   **Cooking time**: 1 hour and 10 minutes   **Portions: 4 people**

Ingredients:

- ✓ Cooking spray
- ✓ 1 large onion, coarsely chopped
- ✓ 2 large carrots, peeled and roughly chopped
- ✓ 2 large celery stalks (with leaves), roughly chopped
- ✓ 1 parsnip, peeled and roughly chopped

Ingredients:

- ✓ 5 cloves of garlic, crushed
- ✓ 1 leek, well cleaned and coarsely chopped
- ✓ 9 cups of water
- ✓ 2 bay leaves
- ✓ 2 teaspoons of sea salt
- ❖ Add the water, bay leaf and salt. Simmer for 1 hour.
- ❖ Remove from the heat and cool slightly. Drain the vegetables, leaving only the stock.
- ❖ To serve, add back some of the vegetables if you like and heat the soup to the desired temperature.

Directions:

- ❖ Spray the bottom of a large saucepan with cooking spray. Put the pan over medium-low heat, add the onion and sauté for about 5 minutes, stirring constantly.
- ❖ Add the carrots, celery, parsnips, garlic and leek to the pot. Fry for a further 3 minutes.

63) Creamy clam chowder with mushrooms

Preparation time: 15 minutes   **Cooking time**: 30 minutes   **Portions: 4**

Ingredients:

- For the clams with mushrooms:
- ✓ ½ cup coarsely chopped shiitake mushrooms
- ✓ 1 teaspoon of coconut oil
- ✓ ¼ cup of water
- ✓ ½ teaspoon celery seeds
- For the soup base:
- ✓ ½ medium onion, chopped
- ✓ 3 medium-sized carrots, peeled and chopped
- ✓ 2 stalks of celery, finely chopped

Ingredients:

- ✓ 1 teaspoon dried thyme
- ✓ 3 cups vegetable stock
- ✓ 1 sheet of nori, finely crumbled
- ✓ For the cream base:
- ✓ 1 cup lightly steamed cauliflower
- ✓ ¾ cup of unsweetened almond milk
- ✓ ¼ teaspoon of sea salt

Directions:

- ❖ To make clams with mushrooms
- ❖ In a large saucepan over medium-high heat, add the mushrooms and coconut oil. Sauté for 3 minutes. Add the water and celery seeds, stirring until the water is absorbed.
- ❖ Remove from the heat and transfer the mushrooms to a plate.
- ❖ To make the soup base
- ❖ In the same pot, over a medium heat, sauté the onion, carrots, celery and thyme for about 5 minutes, or until the onion is softened. Add a little stock if necessary.

- ❖ Then, add the remaining stock and nori and bring to the boil.
- ❖ To make the cream base
- ❖ In a blender or food processor, add the cauliflower, almond milk and salt. Blend to combine. If the mixture is too thick, add a little soup base to thin it out. Blend until the mixture is smooth.
- ❖ To assemble the fish soup
- ❖ Add the mushroom mix and the cream base to the soup base. Stir well to combine.
- ❖ Heat for 5 minutes, or until hot, and serve.

64) Bok choy soup, broccolini and brown rice

Preparation time: 5 minutes   **Cooking time**: 10 minutes   **Portions: 2**

Ingredients:

- ✓ 3 cups vegetable stock
- ✓ 1 cup of chopped bok choy

Ingredients:

- ✓ 1 bunch of broccolini, roughly chopped
- ✓ ½ cup cooked brown rice

Directions:

- ❖ In a medium saucepan over medium heat, place the stock, bok choy, broccolini and brown rice. Bring to the boil and cook for 10 minutes, or until the vegetables are cooked through and tender. Serve.

65) Apple and sweet pumpkin soup

Preparation time: 5 minutes   **Cooking time**: 25 minutes   Serves 2

Ingredients:

- ✓ 1 medium apple, core and slices
- ✓ ½ cup chopped fennel
- ✓ 1½ cups of water, divided
- ✓ 1 cup unsweetened canned pumpkin puree
- ✓ ¾ cup low-sodium vegetable broth
- ✓ 4 small, pitted dates
- ✓ 2 teaspoons of freshly grated ginger or 2 cubes of frozen ginger

Ingredients:

- ✓ ¼ teaspoon ground cinnamon
- ✓ ¼ teaspoon of curry powder
- ✓ ⅛ teaspoon dried thyme
- ✓ ⅛ teaspoon of sea salt
- ✓ ⅛ teaspoon of ground cumin
- ✓ 4 teaspoons of sultanas, for garnish
- ✓ 2 teaspoons of fennel seeds, toasted, for garnish
- ❖ Pour the soup into two bowls and cover each with 2 teaspoons of sultanas and 1 teaspoon of toasted fennel seeds.
- ❖ Serve immediately or allow to cool and serve at room temperature.

Directions:

- ❖ In a saucepan, combine the apples, fennel and ½ cup water. Cover and simmer for about 25 minutes, until the apples and fennel are softened.
- ❖ In a food processor, combine the apple and fennel mixture, pumpkin, remaining 1 cup water, stock, dates, ginger, cinnamon, curry powder, thyme, salt and cumin. Process until reduced to a puree.

66) Tomato and carrot soup with lemon

Preparation time: 5 minutes   **Cooking time**: 35 minutes   Portions: 2

Ingredients:

- ✓ 1 (15-ounce / 425-g) may no sodium added diced tomatoes, drained
- ✓ ¾ cup chopped carrots
- ✓ 1 tablespoon avocado oil
- ✓ ¼ teaspoon of sea salt

Ingredients:

- ✓ 1 cup of water
- ✓ ½ cup low-sodium vegetable broth
- ✓ 2 tablespoons fresh coriander, chopped
- ✓ 1 tablespoon freshly squeezed lemon juice
- ❖ Cook the tomato and carrot mixture for 35 minutes, or until caramelised, then carefully transfer to a food processor.
- ❖ Add the water and stock and whisk until smooth.
- ❖ Garnish with coriander and add lemon juice to taste.

Directions:

- ❖ Preheat the oven to 400ºF (205ºC).
- ❖ In a glass baking dish, combine the tomatoes, carrots, oil and salt and mix well.

67) Courgette and avocado soup with basil

Preparation time: 5 minutes   **Cooking time**: 0 minutes   Serves 2

Ingredients:

- ✓ 2 large courgettes, chopped
- ✓ 1 medium avocado
- ✓ 1 medium pepper
- ✓ ½ cup low-sodium vegetable broth
- ✓ ½ cup of water
- ✓ ¼ cup chopped fennel

Ingredients:

- ✓ 6 fresh basil leaves, plus 2 small leaves for garnish
- ✓ 2 teaspoons fresh rosemary, chopped
- ✓ 1 clove of garlic, peeled, or 1 frozen garlic cube
- ✓ ⅛ teaspoon of sea salt
- ✓ 1½ teaspoons of hulled pumpkin seeds, toasted, for garnish
- ❖ Pour the soup into bowls. Garnish each with a small basil leaf and pumpkin seeds and serve.

Directions:

- ❖ In a high-speed blender or food processor, combine the courgettes, avocado, pepper, stock, water, fennel, basil, rosemary, garlic and salt and blend until pureed.

68) Courgette, spinach and quinoa soup

Preparation time: 5 minutes   **Cooking time**: 25 minutes   **Portions: 4 people**

Ingredients:

- ✓ 2 tablespoons of avocado oil
- ✓ ¼ teaspoon dried oregano
- ✓ ¼ teaspoon dried thyme
- ✓ ⅛ teaspoon of sea salt
- ✓ 1 large onion, chopped
- ✓ 2 large courgettes, peeled and cut into pieces

Directions:

- ❖ In a soup pot, heat the oil over medium heat for 1 minute, then add the oregano, thyme and salt and cook for 30 seconds.
- ❖ Add the onion, cover and cook for 7-8 minutes, stirring regularly, until softened.
- ❖ Add the courgettes. Cook for a further 12 minutes, or until the courgettes are soft.

Ingredients:

- ✓ 1 cup of low-sodium vegetable broth
- ✓ 1 cup of water
- ✓ 1 cup baby spinach
- ✓ 6 large fresh basil leaves
- ✓ ⅓ cup of cooked quinoa (optional)
- ✓ Juice of 1 lemon
- ❖ Add the stock and water and cook for a further 3 minutes, until heated through.
- ❖ Add the spinach and basil and cook until just wilted.
- ❖ Transfer the mixture to a food processor and process until it is pureed.
- ❖ Add quinoa (if using). Season with lemon juice and serve.

69) Easy Cilantro Lime Quinoa.

Preparation time: 5 minutes   **Cooking time:** 15 minutes   **Portions: 6**

Ingredients:

- ✓ 1 cup quinoa, rinsed and draned.
- ✓ ½ cup fresh cilantro, chopped
- ✓ 1 lime zest, grated

Directions:

- ❖ Add quinoa and water to the instant pot and stir well.
- ❖ Seal with a lid and select manual mode and set the timer for 5 minutes.

Ingredients:

- ✓ 2 tbsp. fresh lime juice
- ✓ 1 ¼ cup distilled water feed Sea sa sa
- ❖ Once finished, allow pressure naturally release that open thed.
- ❖ Stir in water, leave to rest.
- ❖ Season with salt and serve.

70) Spinach Quinoa

Preparation time: 10 minutes   **Cooking time:** 25 minutes   **Portions: 4**

Ingredients:

- ✓ 1 cup quinoa
- ✓ 2 cups fresh spinach, chopped
- ✓ 1 ½ cups filtered alkaline water
- ✓ 1 sweet potato, peeled and cut into pieces
- ✓ 1 tsp. coriander powder
- ✓ 1 teaspoon turmandine
- ✓ 1 teaspoon of cumin seds

Directions:

- ❖ Add oil il instant pot and set the sauté mode.
- ❖ Add onion in olive oil and fry for 2 minutes otil onion is softened.
- ❖ Add garlic, ginger, spices and quinoa and coook for 3-4 minutes.
- ❖ Add spinach, sweet potatoes, and water and stir well.

Ingredients:

- ✓ 1 tsp. fresh ginger, chopped
- ✓ 2 garlic cloves, chopped
- ✓ 1 onion cut in half
- ✓ 2 tbsp olive oil
- ✓ 1 fresh lime juice
- ✓ Pepper Salt
- ❖ Cook at high pressure for 2 minutes.
- ❖ When it's finished, release the pressure naturally and then open the container. Add the lime juice and mix well.
- ❖ Serve and enjoy.

71) Healthy broccoli Asparagus Soup

Preparation time: 15 minutes.   **Cooking time:** 28 minutes.   **Portions: 6**

Ingredients:

- ✓ 2 cups broccoli florets, chopped
- ✓ 15 asparages spears, escreated and chopped
- ✓ 1 tsp. dried oregano
- ✓ 1 tbsp. fresh thyme leaves
- ✓ ½ cup unsweetened almond milk

Directions:

- ❖ Add the oil to the bowl and stir the bowl.
- ❖ Add onion to olive oil and fry until onion is softened.
- ❖ Add the garlic and leave to stand for 30 minutes.
- ❖ Add all the vegetables and salt and dry well.

Ingredients:

- ✓ 3 ½ cups filtered alkaline water
- ✓ 2 cups cauliflower florets, chopped
- ✓ 2 tsp. garlic, chopped 1 cup onion, chopped
- ✓ 2 tbsp. olive oil
- ✓ Salt Pepper
- ❖ Seal pot with lid and coook on manual mode for 3 minutes.
- ❖ Once finished, you can rinse to minimise pressure and then close the container.
- ❖ Puree the soup with an immersion blender until smooth. Add the almond milk, herbs, pepper and salt.
- ❖ Serve and enjoy.

72) Creamy Asparagus Soup

Preparation time: 10 minutes   **Cooking time:** 40 minutes   **Portions: 6**

Ingredients:

- ✓ 2 lbs. fresh asparagus cut off woody stems
- ✓ ¼ tablespoon lemon zest
- ✓ 2 tbsp. lime juice
- ✓ 14 oz. coconut milk
- ✓ 1 tsp. tied thyme.
- ✓ ½ tsp. oregano
- ✓ ½ tsp. sage

Directions:

- ❖ Preheat the oven to 400ºF/ 200ºC.
- ❖ The paper tray with the scraps and leftovers.
- ❖ Arrange the asparagus spears on a baking tray. Add 2 tbsp of walnut oil and add salt, seasonings, garlic and sugar.
- ❖ Kiss it with a dose of 20-25 mnutes.
- ❖ Add the remaining oil in the instant pot and set the pot on sauté mode.
- ❖ Add the garlic and milk to the pot and fry for 2-3 minutes.

Ingredients:

- ✓ 1 ½ cups alkaline water filtered.
- ✓ 1 Head of a hunting dog coming out of the floor.
- ✓ 1 tablespoon. garlic, minced
- ✓ 1 leek, sliced
- ✓ 3 tbsp. coconut oil
- ✓ Pinch of Himalayan salt.
- ❖ Add the cauliflower florets and water to the bowl and mix well.
- ❖ Insert the cooker with a rod and select steam and let it stand for 4 minutes.
- ❖ When finished, release the pressure using the quick-release method.
- ❖ Add roasted asparagus, lime zest, lime juice, and coco milk and stir well.
- ❖ Puree the soup with an immersion blender until it is pureed.
- ❖ Serve and have fun

73) Spicy Eggplant

Preparation time: 15 minutes   **Cooking time:** 5 minutes   **Portions: 4**

Ingredients:

- ✓ 1 aubergine, cut into 1inch cubes
- ✓ ½ cup filtered alkaline water
- ✓ 1 life, in book form.
- ✓ ½ tsp. Italian seasoning
- ✓ 1 tsp. paprika

Directions:

- ❖ Add the extract and salt to the instant flour.
- ❖ Cook on manual high pressure for 5 minutes.
- ❖ When finished, rinse with peanut butter and then milk. Wet the aubergines well.

Ingredients:

- ✓ ½ tsp. red pepper
- ✓ 1 tsp. garlic powder
- ✓ 2 tbsp. olive oil extra virgin
- ✓ ¼ teaspoon of sea salt
- ❖ Add oil to the Instant Pot and set pot on sauté mode.
- ❖ Put the ingredient back into the pot with the chopper, garlic, paprika and salt and mix until it is included.
- ❖ Coook on sauté mode for 5 minutes. Stir from time to time.
- ❖ Serve enjoy.

74) Brussels Sprouts and carrots

Preparation time: 10 minutes   **Cooking time:** 5 minutes   **Portions: 6**

Ingredients:

- ✓ 1 ½ pounds of Brussels sprouts, trimmed and cut alf
- ✓ 4 carrots peel and cut slices are shaped like a knife.
- ✓ 1 tsp. olive oil
- ✓ ½ cup filtered alkaline water
- ✓ 1 tbsp. dried parsley

Directions:

- ❖ Add all ingredients to the instant pot and mix well.
- ❖ Put the lid on the pan and cook over a high heat for 2 minutes.

Ingredients:

- ✓ ¼ tsp. garlic, minced
- ✓ ¼ tsp. pepper
- ✓ ¼ tsp. sea salt

- ❖ When finished, rinse with the quick-release button and then with the lid.
- ❖ Stir well all serve.

75) Matured Cajun Zucchini

Preparation time: 8 minutes.   **Cooking time:** 2 minutes.   **Portions: 2**

Ingredients:

- ✓ 4 zucchinis, sliced
- ✓ 1 tsp. garlic powder
- ✓ 1 tsp. paprika

Directions:

- ❖ Add all the ingredients to the pot and mix well.
- ❖ Close the cooker with the lid and cook at low pressure for 1 minute.

Ingredients:

- ✓ 2 tbsp. Cajun seasoning
- ✓ ½ cup melted milk water
- ✓ 1 tablespoon olive oil
- ❖ Once finished, release the pressure using the quick-release method then opene the lid.
- ❖ Mix well and serve.

- ❖ 130 Fat: 7.9 Carbohydrates: 14.7 g. Sugar: 7.2 g. Protein: 5.3 g. Cholesterol: 0 mg.

76) Fried cabage

Preparation time: 10 minutes   **Cooking time:** 3 minutes   **Portions: 6**

Ingredients:

- ✓ 1 head cabbage, chopped
- ✓ ½ teaspoon of olive oil
- ✓ ½ onion, diced
- ✓ ½ tsp. paprika

Directions:

- ❖ Add olive oil il inside the Instant Pot and set the sauté mode.
- ❖ Add onion in olive oil and sauté until soft.
- ❖ Add the ingredients for preparation and the product for packaging.

Ingredients:

- ✓ 1 onion, chopped
- ✓ 1 fibreglass basket
- ✓ 2 tbsp. olive oil
- ✓ ½ tbsp sea salt
- ❖ Close the lid and cook over a high heat for 3 minutes.
- ❖ When you're finished, release the pressure using the quick-release method then open the lids.
- ❖ Mix well and serve.

77) Tofu Curry

Preparation time: 10 minutes   **Cooking time:** 4 hours   **Portions: 4**

Ingredients:

- ✓ 1 cup firm tofu, diced
- ✓ 2 tbsp garlic cloves, minced
- ✓ 1 onion, chopped
- ✓ 8 oz. tomato pured
- ✓ 2 cups pepper, chopped

Directions:

- ❖ Add all ingredients except tofu in a blender and blend until smooth.
- ❖ Put the blended mixture into the Instant Pot.

Ingredients:

- ✓ 1 tablespoon garm masala
- ✓ 2 tbsp. olive oil
- ✓ 1 tablespoon peanut butter
- ✓ 10 oz. coconut milk
- ✓ 1 ½ tsp. sea salt
- ❖ Add the tofu to a bowl and dry it well.
- ❖ Seal pot with a lid and select slow coook mode and set the timer for 4 hours.
- ❖ Mix well and serve.

78) Cauliflower with sauce

Preparation time: 10 minutes   **Cooking time**: 15 minutes   **Portions: 5**

Ingredients:

- ✓ 1 large bed cauliflower head, cut bottom leaves
  For marinade:
- ✓ 1 tsp. paprika ½ tbsp olive oil
- ✓ Tbsp. fresh parsley, chopped
- ✓ 1 tbsp. thyme fresh
- ✓ 3 garlic cloves
- ✓ Salt Pepper

Directions:

- ❖ In a full bowl, mix all the marinade ingredints.
- ❖ Rub the marinade evenly over the entire head of the cauliflower.
- ❖ For gravy: add oil instant pot and set the pot on sauté modeuté.
- ❖ Add the garlic and onion in oil olive oil and sauté until the onion is softened.
- ❖ Add the water, lemon juice and thyme and stir.
- ❖ Place the trivet in the Instant Pot. Place the cauliflower in the trivet.

Ingredients:

For gravy:
- ✓ ½ tbsp. lime juice
- ✓ ½ teaspoon
- ✓ 1 ½ cups filtered alkaline water
- ✓ 2 cloves garlic
- ✓ 1 tsp. olive oil
- ✓ 1 onion, diced
- ❖ Seal the pot with lid and coook on manual high pressure for 3 minutes.
- ❖ When finished, allow to release naturally pressure for 5 minutes then release using a quick-release method. Transfer the cauliflower head to a serving dish and salt for 3-4 minutes.
- ❖ Reduce the Instant Pot to a puree with an immersion blender until it reaches consistency.
- ❖ Put some of the herb on a frying pan and cook the meat for 3-4 minutes.
- ❖ Serve the cauliflower with gravy.

79) Zucchini Noodles

Preparation time: 8 minutes   **Cooking time**: 2 minutes   **Portions: 2**

Ingredients:

- ✓ 2 large courgettes, spiralised
- ✓ 1 tbsp. fresh mint leaves, sliced
- ✓ 1/3 lime juice
- ✓ ½ lime zest

Directions:

- ❖ Add oil instant pot and seet the pot outé.
- ❖ Add the lime zest, garlic and salt to the olive oil and leave to dry for 30 minutes.

Ingredients:

- ✓ 2 garlic cloves, chopped
- ✓ 2 tbsp. olive oil
- ✓ ¼ tsp. pepper
- ✓ ½ tsp. sea salt
- ❖ Add the zucchini noodles and lime juice and stir for 30 seconds. Season with pepper and salt. Season with milk.
- ❖ Serve and enjoy.

80) Buckwheat Porridge

Preparation time: 20 minutes   **Cooking time**: 10 minutes   **Portions: 4**

Ingredients:

- ✓ 1 cup buckwheat groats, rinsed
- ✓ 2 tablespoons almonds, chopped
- ✓ ½ tsp. vanilla

Directions:

- ❖ Add the peanut butter, vanilla, cinnamon and milk to the instant water and mix well.
- ❖ Close the cooker with the lid and cook at manual high pressure for 6 minutes.

Ingredients:

- ✓ 1 tsp. cinnamon
- ✓ 3 cups untreated almond milk
- ✓ 4-5 drops liquid stevia.
- ❖ Once finished, let release pressure naturally then open the lid.
- ❖ Top with chopped almonds and serve.

81) Vegetable soup

Preparation time: 15 minutes

Cooking time: 25 minutes

Portions: 3

Ingredients:

- ✓ ½ tablespoon olive oil
- ✓ 2 tablespoons chopped onion
- ✓ 2 teaspoons of minced garlic
- ✓ ½ cup of carrots, peeled and chopped
- ✓ ½ cup of green cabbage, chopped
- ✓ 1/3 cup French beans, mashed

Ingredients:

- ✓ 3 cups of homemade vegetable stock
- ✓ ½ tablespoon fresh lemon juice
- ✓ 3 tablespoons of water
- ✓ 2 tablespoons arrowroot starch
- ✓ Sea salt and freshly ground black pepper, to taste

Directions:

- ❖ Heat the oil in a large heavy-bottomed frying pan over medium heat and fry the onion and garlic for about 4-5 minutes.
- ❖ Add the carrots, cabbage and beans and cook for about 4-5 minutes, stirring frequently.
- ❖ Stir in the broth and bring to the boil.
- ❖ Cook for about 4-5 minutes.

- ❖ Meanwhile, in a small bowl, dissolve the arrowroot starch in water.
- ❖ Slowly add the arrowroot starch mixture, stirring constantly.
- ❖ Cook for about 7-8 minutes, stirring occasionally.
- ❖ Add the lemon juice, salt and black pepper and remove from the heat.
- ❖ Serve hot.

82) Lentil and spinach soup

Preparation time: 15 minutes

Cooking time: 1¼ hours Total time: 1½ hoursPayments

Portions: 6

Ingredients:

- ✓ 2 tablespoons of olive oil
- ✓ 2 carrots, peeled and cut into pieces
- ✓ 2 stalks of celery, chopped
- ✓ 2 sweet onions, chopped
- ✓ 3 cloves of garlic, minced
- ✓ 1½ cups brown lentils, rinsed
- ✓ 2 cups of tomatoes, finely chopped
- ✓ ¼ teaspoon dried basil, crushed
- ✓ ¼ teaspoon dried oregano, crushed
- ✓ ¼ teaspoon dried thyme, crushed

Ingredients:

- ✓ 1 teaspoon ground cumin
- ✓ ½ teaspoon ground coriander
- ✓ ½ teaspoon of paprika
- ✓ 6 cups of vegetable stock
- ✓ 3 cups fresh spinach, chopped
- ✓ Sea salt and freshly ground black pepper, to taste
- ✓ 2 tablespoons fresh lemon juice

Directions:

- ❖ In a large soup pot, heat the oil over medium heat and sauté the carrot, celery and onion for about 5 minutes.
- ❖ Add the garlic and fry for about 1 minute.
- ❖ Add the lentils and fry for about 3 minutes.
- ❖ Stir in the tomatoes, herbs, spices and stock and bring to the boil.

- ❖ Reduce the heat to low and simmer, partially covered, for about 1 hour or until cooked to perfection.
- ❖ Add the spinach, salt and black pepper and cook for about 4 minutes.
- ❖ Add the lemon juice and remove from the heat.
- ❖ Serve hot.

83) Vegetarian stew

Preparation time: 20 minutes

Cooking time: 35 minutes

Portions: 8

Ingredients:

- ✓ 2 tablespoons of coconut oil
- ✓ 1 large sweet onion, chopped
- ✓ 1 medium parsnip, peeled and chopped
- ✓ 3 tablespoons of homemade tomato paste
- ✓ 2 large cloves of garlic, minced
- ✓ ½ teaspoon ground cinnamon
- ✓ ½ teaspoon ground ginger
- ✓ 1 teaspoon ground cumin
- ✓ ¼ teaspoon cayenne pepper

Ingredients:

- ✓ 2 medium-sized carrots, peeled and chopped
- ✓ 2 medium purple potatoes, peeled and cut into pieces
- ✓ 2 medium sweet potatoes, peeled and cut into pieces
- ✓ 4 cups of homemade vegetable stock
- ✓ 2 cups fresh cabbage, cut and chopped
- ✓ 2 tablespoons fresh lemon juice
- ✓ Sea salt and freshly ground black pepper, to taste

Directions:

- ❖ In a large soup pot, melt the coconut oil over medium-high heat and sauté the onion for about 5 minutes.
- ❖ Add the parsnips and fry for about 3 minutes.
- ❖ Stir in the tomato paste, garlic and spices and fry for about 2 minutes.

- ❖ Stir in the carrots, potatoes, sweet potatoes and stock and bring to the boil.
- ❖ Reduce the heat to medium-low and simmer covered for about 20 minutes.
- ❖ Add the cabbage, lemon juice, salt and black pepper and simmer for about 5 minutes.
- ❖ Serve hot.

84) Alka-Goulash fast

Preparation time: **Cooking time:**   **Portions: 4**

Ingredients:
- ✓ 1 onion, finely chopped
- ✓ 1 clove of garlic, crushed
- ✓ 2 carrots, diced
- ✓ 3 courgettes, diced
- ✓ 2 tablespoons of olive oil
- ✓ 1 tablespoon paprika
- ✓ 1/4 teaspoon ground nutmeg

Directions:
- ❖ Fry the onion, garlic, carrot and courgette in olive oil over a medium heat for 5 minutes, until softened.
- ❖ Add paprika, nutmeg, parsley and tomato puree.

Ingredients:
- ✓ 1 tablespoon fresh parsley, chopped
- ✓ 1 tablespoon of tomato puree
- ✓ 2 cups tomatoes, peeled
- ✓ 2 cups of cooked, drained and rinsed red beans
- ✓ 1/2 cup of tomato juice
- ✓ Salt and black pepper to taste

- ❖ Add the tomatoes, red beans and tomato juice and mix.
- ❖ Simmer for 10 minutes until heated through.
- ❖ Serve immediately. Enjoy your meal!

85) Pea risotto

Preparation time: **Cooking time:**   **Portions: 4**

Ingredients:
- ✓ 1 vegetable stock cube
- ✓ 2 tablespoons of olive oil
- ✓ 1 onion, finely chopped
- ✓ 3 cloves of garlic, finely chopped
- ✓ 1 cup basmati rice

Directions:
- ❖ Crumble the vegetable stock cube into 3 cups of boiling water. Let it dissolve and then reduce the heat.
- ❖ Thaw the peas in hot water, drain them and set them aside for later.
- ❖ Season the onion with salt and black pepper to taste, and then fry in olive oil over medium heat for about 5 minutes, until softened.
- ❖ Add the garlic to the pan and fry it for a few minutes, taking care not to burn it.
- ❖ Add the rice to the pan and stir well. Pour in a little vegetable stock so that the rice is barely covered.

Ingredients:
- ✓ 1 cup frozen peas
- ✓ 1 cup of fresh spinach leaves
- ✓ 1 lemon, grated and squeezed
- ✓ Salt and black pepper to taste
- ✓ 3 cups of water
- ❖ Simmer over a medium heat, stirring constantly, for several minutes, until the liquid has been almost completely absorbed.
- ❖ Add the rest of the stock one ladle at a time, stirring constantly until each batch of stock has been absorbed.
- ❖ When each ladleful has been absorbed and the rice is fully cooked, add the defrosted peas, spinach leaves and lemon juice.
- ❖ Stir until the spinach leaves are wilted and serve hot.
- ❖ Have fun!

86) Satisfying lunch smoothie Alka

Preparation time: **Cooking time:**   **Portions: 1-2**

Ingredients:
- ✓ 1 large avocado
- ✓ 1.5 cup of coconut or almond milk
- ✓ 2 tablespoons of fresh coriander leaves
- ✓ 2 tablespoons of coconut oil

Directions:
- ❖ Simply blend all the ingredients except the seeds and oil.

Ingredients:
- ✓ 1 lemon, squeezed
- ✓ 4 tablespoons of chia seeds
- ✓ Himalayan salt to taste

- ❖ Stir well, add the chia seeds and enjoy with Himalayan salt.
- ❖ Have fun!

87) Alkaline pizza bread

Preparation time:

Cooking time:

Portions: 1

Ingredients:
- ✓ Linseed, 100g
- ✓ Sunflower seeds, 200g
- ✓ Pepper, a pinch
- ✓ Dried tomatoes, 50g

Ingredients:
- ✓ Organic salt or sea salt, a pinch
- ✓ Extra virgin olive oil (cold pressed), 4 teaspoons
- ✓ Optional: Fresh wild garlic

Directions:
- ❖ Note: You need to soak the sunflower seeds for at least four hours.
- ❖ Blend the flax seeds in a blender until they are reduced to a powder.
- ❖ Once the sunflower seeds have lasted up to four hours, put them in a blender and blend them for a few seconds.

- ❖ Now add all the ingredients into a bowl.
- ❖ Using your hands, form a dough until it reaches the right consistency.
- ❖ The idea is to form a couple of pizza/bread crusts.
- ❖ Place them in a dehydrator or oven and dehydrate for up to twelve hours. Serve.

88) Alkaline-filled avocado

Preparation time:

Cooking time:

Portions:

Ingredients:
- ✓ Oregano, 1 teaspoon
- ✓ Ripe avocado, 1
- ✓ Lime juice (fresh), 1 teaspoon
- ✓ Fresh basil, 1 teaspoon

Ingredients:
- ✓ Chopped onions, 1 teaspoon
- ✓ Tomato, ½
- ✓ Extra virgin olive oil (cold pressed), 4 teaspoons
- ✓ Pepper and sea salt
- ❖ Mix the olive oil, chopped onion, lime juice and chopped tomato and put it in the holes of the avocado.

Directions:
- ❖ Cut the avocado into two equal halves and remove the seed.
- ❖ Use salt and pepper to season both halves.

- ❖ Sprinkle with oregano and basil and serve.

89) Alkaline potato salad

Preparation time:

Cooking time:

Portions: 4

Ingredients:
- ✓ Cauliflower, 1 cup
- ✓ Dill, 2 tablespoons
- ✓ Vegenaise, 1 teaspoon
- ✓ Red onion, 1
- ✓ Cucumber (small), 1
- ✓ Broccoli, 2 cups

Ingredients:
- ✓ Green/red pepper (small), 1
- ✓ Red potatoes, 600g
- ✓ Juice of 1 lemon
- ✓ Sea salt
- ✓ Olive oil (cold pressed), 3 tablespoons

Directions:
- ❖ Steam the cauliflower and broccoli for a few minutes and make sure they are crispy.
- ❖ Also, steam the potatoes until they are slightly soft and let them cool.
- ❖ Once they have cooled, slice the potatoes but do not remove the skin and throw them into a large bowl.
- ❖ Then, add the chopped cucumber, cauliflower, pepper, broccoli, dill, finely chopped onion and salt.

- ❖ Mix well and set aside.
- ❖ Take a small bowl and mix the veganaise, olive oil and lemon juice until smooth.
- ❖ Stir it into the potato salad and mix gently.
- ❖ It can be served immediately, but it is better to set it aside for a few hours (because it tastes better that way).
- ❖ You are free to add other seasonings according to your taste.

90) Almonds with sautéed vegetables

Preparation time: **Cooking time**:   **Portions: 4**

Ingredients:
- ✓ Young beans, 150g
- ✓ Broccoli florets, 4
- ✓ Oregano and cumin, ½ teaspoon
- ✓ Lemon juice (fresh), 3 tablespoons
- ✓ Garlic clove (finely chopped), 1

Directions:
- ❖ Add the broccoli, beans and other vegetables to a large frying pan and fry until the beans and broccoli turn dark green.
- ❖ Make sure that the vegetables are also crispy.
- ❖ Now add the chopped garlic and onion, fry and stir for a few minutes.

Ingredients:
- ✓ Cauliflower, 1 cup
- ✓ Olive oil (cold pressed), 4 tablespoons
- ✓ Pepper and salt to taste
- ✓ Some soaked almonds (sliced), for garnish
- ✓ Yellow onion, 1
- ❖ Then, put the seasoning together.
- ❖ Take a small bowl, add the lemon juice, oregano, cumin and oil and mix well.
- ❖ Add some vegetables, stir slowly and taste for pepper and salt.
- ❖ Finally, use the sliced almonds as a garnish.
- ❖ Serve.

91) Alkaline sweet potato mash

Preparation time: **Cooking time**:   **Portions: 3-4**

Ingredients:
- ✓ Sea salt, 1 tablespoon
- ✓ Curry powder, ½ table spoon
- ✓ Sweet potatoes (large), 6

Directions:
- ❖ First, take a large mixing bowl.
- ❖ Wash and cut the sweet potatoes and add them to the cooking pot and cook for about twenty minutes.

Ingredients:
- ✓ Coconut milk (fresh), 1 ½ - 2 cups
- ✓ Extra virgin olive oil (cold pressed), 1 tablespoon
- ✓ Pepper, 1 pinch
- ❖ Then, remove the sweet potatoes and mash them to the desired consistency.
- ❖ Finally, all you have to do is add the remaining ingredients and serve.

92) Mediterranean peppers

Preparation time: **Cooking time**:   **Portions: 2**

Ingredients:
- ✓ Oregano, 1 teaspoon
- ✓ Garlic cloves (crushed), 2
- ✓ Fresh parsley (chopped), 2 tablespoons
- ✓ Vegetable bouillon (without yeast), 1 cup
- ✓ Provincial herbs, 1 teaspoon

Directions:
- ❖ Heat the olive oil in a frying pan over medium heat, add the pepper and onions and stir.
- ❖ Add the garlic and stir.

Ingredients:
- ✓ Red pepper (sliced) 2 + Yellow pepper (sliced) 2
- ✓ Red onions (thinly sliced), 2 medium-sized
- ✓ Extra virgin olive oil (cold pressed), 2 tablespoons
- ✓ Salt and pepper to taste

- ❖ Then, add the vegetable stock and season with parsley and herbs, as well as pepper and salt to taste.
- ❖ Cover the pan and leave to cook for fourteen to fifteen minutes.
- ❖ Serve.

93) Tomato and avocado sauce with potatoes

Preparation time: **Cooking time**:   **Portions: 3**

Ingredients:
- ✓ Red onion 1
- ✓ 2 Tomatoes
- ✓ ½ - 1 lemon (squeezed)
- ✓ Chives (fresh and chopped), 1 teaspoon
- ✓ Parsley (fresh and chopped), 1 teaspoon

Directions:
- ❖ Take a pan and cook the potatoes in salted water, (cook the potatoes with the skin intact).
- ❖ Then, peel the avocado, throw it into a bowl and mash it with a fork.

Ingredients:
- ✓ Cayenne pepper, ½ teaspoon
- ✓ Avocado (ripe), 2
- ✓ Waxy potatoes (medium size), 6
- ✓ Saltwater
- ✓ Pepper and salt
- ❖ Now, dice the onion and tomatoes and add them to the bowl along with the parsley, chives and cayenne.
- ❖ Mix well and season with pepper, lemon juice and salt.
- ❖ Serve together with the potatoes.

94) **Alkaline beans and coconut**

Preparation time: **Cooking time:** **Portions: 4**

Ingredients:

- ✓ Ground cumin, ½ teaspoon
- ✓ Red chilli pepper (crushed), 1-2
- ✓ Coconut milk (fresh), 3 tablespoons
- ✓ Dry flaked coconut, 1 tablespoon
- ✓ Garlic (chopped), 2 cloves
- ✓ Cayenne pepper, 1 pinch

Directions:

- ❖ Heat the oil in a frying pan and add the beans, cumin, garlic, ginger and glaze and fry for about six minutes.

Ingredients:

- ✓ Sea salt, 1 pinch
- ✓ Extra virgin olive oil (cold pressed), 3 tablespoons
- ✓ Fresh herbs of your choice, 1 teaspoon
- ✓ One (1) pound of green beans, cut into 1-inch pieces
- ✓ Fresh ginger (chopped), ½ teaspoon

- ❖ Add the coconut flakes and oil and fry until the milk is fully cooked (this can take three or four minutes).
- ❖ Season with pepper, salt and herbs to taste. Serve.

95) **Alkaline vegetable lasagne**

Preparation time: **Cooking time:** **Portions: 1**

Ingredients:

- ✓ Parsley root, 1
- ✓ Leek (small), 1
- ✓ Radish (small), 1
- ✓ Corn salad, 1
- ✓ Tomatoes (large), 3
- ✓ Garlic, 1 clove

Directions:

- ❖ Take a blender and add the lemon juice, the garlic clove and the avocado.
- ❖ Cut the pepper into thin strips, cut the leek into thin rings and finely grate the parsley root and radish. When you have finished, mix everything with the avocado cream.

Ingredients:

- ✓ Avocado (soft), 2
- ✓ Lemon (squeezed), 1-2
- ✓ Rocket, 1
- ✓ Parsley (a few)
- ✓ Red pepper, 1

- ❖ We start with the first layer of the lasagne.
- ❖ Place the corn salad in a casserole dish, add the avocado spread well.
- ❖ For the second layer, add the sliced tomatoes.
- ❖ Finally, add the rocket and parsley for the final layer.
- ❖ Serve.

96) Aloo Gobi

Preparation time: **Cooking time:**   **Servings: 1 bowl**

Ingredients:

- ✓ Cauliflower, 750g
- ✓ Fresh ginger, 20g
- ✓ Large onions, 2
- ✓ Mint, 1/3 cup
- ✓ Turmeric, 2 teaspoons
- ✓ Diced tomatoes, 400g
- ✓ Fresh garlic, 2 cloves
- ✓ Cayenne pepper, 2 teaspoons

Directions:

- ❖ Blend the chilli, garlic and ginger.
- ❖ Fry the oil in a wok for three minutes and add the onion until golden brown.
- ❖ Add the ground pasta and fry for a few seconds, then add; garam masala, chilli, turmeric, tomatoes and salt.

Ingredients:

- ✓ Cilantro/coriander leaves, 1/3 cup
- ✓ Large potatoes, 4
- ✓ Garam masala, 2 teaspoons
- ✓ Green chilli, 4
- ✓ Water, 3 cups
- ✓ Extra virgin olive oil (cold pressed), 125 ml
- ✓ Salt to taste

- ❖ Cook for about five minutes and add all the other ingredients.
- ❖ Stir for three minutes and add the water.
- ❖ Cook until the sauce is thick.
- ❖ Serve with Basmati rice or as a side dish.

97) Pumpkin smoothie

Preparation time: 10 minutes   **Cooking time:**   **Portions: 2**

Ingredients:

- ✓ 1 cup of homemade pumpkin puree
- ✓ 1 medium banana, peeled and sliced
- ✓ 1 tablespoon maple syrup
- ✓ 1 teaspoon ground linseed

Directions:

- ❖ Place all ingredients in a high-speed blender and pulse until creamy.

Ingredients:

- ✓ ½ teaspoon ground cinnamon
- ✓ ¼ teaspoon ground ginger
- ✓ 1½ cups unsweetened almond milk
- ✓ ¼ cup ice cubes
- ❖ Pour the smoothie into two glasses and serve immediately.

98) Red fruit and vegetable smoothie

Preparation time: 10 minutes   **Cooking time**:   **Portions**: 2

Ingredients:

- ✓ ½ cup of fresh raspberries
- ✓ ½ cup of fresh strawberries
- ✓ ½ red pepper, seeded and chopped
- ✓ ½ cup red cabbage, chopped

Directions:

- ❖ Place all ingredients in a high-speed blender and pulse until creamy.

Ingredients:

- ✓ 1 small tomato
- ✓ 1 cup of water
- ✓ ½ cup of ice cubes

- ❖ Pour the smoothie into two glasses and serve immediately.

99) Kale smoothie

Preparation time: 10 minutes   **Cooking time**:   **Portions**: 2

Ingredients:

- ✓ 3 fresh cabbage stalks, cut and chopped
- ✓ 1-2 celery stalks, chopped
- ✓ ½ avocado, peeled, pitted and chopped

Directions:

- ❖ Place all ingredients in a high-speed blender and pulse until creamy.

Ingredients:

- ✓ ½ inch ginger root, chopped
- ✓ ½ inch turmeric root, chopped
- ✓ 2 cups of coconut milk
- ❖ Pour the smoothie into two glasses and serve immediately.

100) Green tofu smoothie

Preparation time: 10 minutes   **Cooking time**:   **Portions**: 2

Ingredients:

- ✓ 1½ cups cucumber, peeled and roughly chopped
- ✓ 3 cups of fresh spinach
- ✓ 2 cups of frozen broccoli
- ✓ ½ cup of tofu silken, drained and pressed

Directions:

- ❖ Place all ingredients in a high-speed blender and pulse until creamy.

Ingredients:

- ✓ 1 tablespoon fresh lime juice
- ✓ 4-5 drops of liquid stevia
- ✓ 1 cup unsweetened almond milk
- ✓ ½ cup ice, crushed
- ❖ Pour the smoothie into two glasses and serve immediately.

101) Grape and chard smoothie

Preparation time: 10 minutes   **Cooking time**:   **Portions**: 2

Ingredients:

- ✓ 2 cups of seedless green grapes
- ✓ 2 cups fresh beets, cut and chopped
- ✓ 2 tablespoons maple syrup

Directions:

- ❖ Place all ingredients in a high-speed blender and pulse until creamy.

Ingredients:

- ✓ 1 teaspoon fresh lemon juice
- ✓ 1½ cups of water
- ✓ 4 ice cubes
- ❖ Pour the smoothie into two glasses and serve immediately.

102) Matcha Smoothie

Preparation time: 10 minutes   **Cooking time**:   **Portions**: 2

Ingredients:
- ✓ 2 tablespoons of chia seeds
- ✓ 2 teaspoons matcha green tea powder
- ✓ ½ teaspoon fresh lemon juice
- ✓ ½ teaspoon xanthan gum

Directions:
- ❖ Place all ingredients in a high-speed blender and pulse until creamy.

Ingredients:
- ✓ 8-10 drops of liquid stevia
- ✓ 4 tablespoons of coconut cream
- ✓ 1½ cups unsweetened almond milk
- ✓ ¼ cup ice cubes
- ❖ Pour the smoothie into two glasses and serve immediately.

103) Banana smoothie

Preparation time: 10 minutes   **Cooking time**:   **Portions**: 2

Ingredients:
- ✓ 2 cups of cooled unsweetened almond milk
- ✓ 1 large frozen banana, peeled and sliced

Directions:
- ❖ Place all ingredients in a high-speed blender and pulse until creamy.

Ingredients:
- ✓ 1 tablespoon almonds, chopped
- ✓ 1 teaspoon organic vanilla extract
- ❖ Pour the smoothie into two glasses and serve immediately.

104) Strawberry smoothie

Preparation time: 10 minutes   **Cooking time**:   **Portions**: 2

Ingredients:
- ✓ 2 cups of cooled unsweetened almond milk
- ✓ 1½ cups of frozen strawberries

Directions:
- ❖ Add all ingredients to a high-speed blender and pulse until smooth.

Ingredients:
- ✓ 1 banana, peeled and sliced
- ✓ ¼ teaspoon organic vanilla extract
- ❖ Pour the smoothie into two glasses and serve immediately.

105) Raspberry and tofu smoothie

Preparation time: 15 minutes   **Cooking time**:   **Portions**: 2

Ingredients:
- ✓ 1½ cups of fresh raspberries
- ✓ 6 ounces of hard boiled tofu silken, drained
- ✓ 1/8 teaspoon of coconut extract

Directions:
- ❖ Add all ingredients to a high-speed blender and pulse until smooth.

Ingredients:
- ✓ 1 teaspoon stevia powder
- ✓ 1½ cups unsweetened almond milk
- ✓ ¼ cup ice cubes, crushed
- ❖ Pour the smoothie into two glasses and serve immediately.

106) Mango smoothie

Preparation time: 10 minutes   Cooking time: Portions: 2

Ingredients:

- ✓ 2 cups frozen mango, peeled, stoned and chopped
- ✓ ¼ cup almond butter
- ✓ Pinch of ground turmeric

Directions:

- ❖ Add all ingredients to a high-speed blender and pulse until smooth.

Ingredients:

- ✓ 2 tablespoons fresh lemon juice
- ✓ 1¼ cup unsweetened almond milk
- ✓ ¼ cup ice cubes
- ❖ Pour the smoothie into two glasses and serve immediately.

107) Pineapple smoothie

Preparation time: 10 minutes   Cooking time: Portions: 2

Ingredients:

- ✓ 2 cups pineapple, chopped
- ✓ ½ teaspoon fresh ginger, peeled and chopped
- ✓ ½ teaspoon ground turmeric
- ✓ 1 teaspoon of natural immune support supplement*.

Directions:

- ❖ Add all ingredients to a high-speed blender and pulse until smooth.

Ingredients:

- ✓ 1 teaspoon chia seeds
- ✓ 1½ cups of cold green tea
- ✓ ½ cup ice, crushed
- ❖ Pour the smoothie into two glasses and serve immediately.

108) Cabbage and pineapple smoothie

Preparation time: 15 minutes   Cooking time: Portions: 2

Ingredients:

- ✓ 1½ cups fresh cabbage, chopped and shredded
- ✓ 1 frozen banana, peeled and chopped
- ✓ ½ cup of fresh pineapple chunks

Directions:

- ❖ Add all ingredients to a high-speed blender and pulse until smooth.

Ingredients:

- ✓ 1 cup unsweetened coconut milk
- ✓ ½ cup of fresh orange juice
- ✓ ½ cup of ice
- ❖ Pour the smoothie into two glasses and serve immediately.

AUTHOR BIBLIOGRAPHY

THE ESSENCIAL ALKALINE DIET COOKBOOK FOR BEGINNERS

100+ Alkaline Recipes to Bring Your Body Back to Balance! Healthy Recipes to Enjoy Favorite Foods for Weight-Loss!

THE ALKAINE HEALTHY DIET FOR WOMEN

The Effective Way to Follow an Alkaline Diet comprising Plant-Based Diet Recipes: Natural Ways To Prevent Diabetes! 100+ Recipes Included!

THE ALKAINE HEALTHY DIET FOR MEN

100+ Recipes to Understand pH, Eat Well, and Reclaim Your Health! Plant-Based Recipes Are Included! Boost your Weight-Loss!

THE ALKAINE HEALTHY DIET FOR KIDS

100+ Recipes for Your Health, To Lose Weight Naturally and Bring Your Body Back To Balance

THE ALKALINE FIET COOKBOOK FOR ONE

100+ Recipes to Lose Weight and Get the Benefits of an Alkaline Diet - Alkaline Smoothies Included for Your Way to Vibrant Health - Massive Energy and Natural Weight Loss! Plant-Based Recipes Are Included!

THE ALKAINE DIET FOR WOMEN AFTER 50

2 Books in 1: The Complete Alkaline Diet Guidebook for Beginners: Understand pH, Eat Well with Easy Alkaline Diet Cookbook and more than 200+ Delicious Recipes (Lose weight, Beginners, Foods & Diet, Reset Cleanse)

THE SPECIAL ALKALINE DIET FOR TWO

2 Books in 1: Guidebook for Beginners: Understand pH, Eat Well with Easy Alkaline Diet Cookbook and more than 200 Delicious Recipes! Plant-Based Recipes Are Included!

THE ALKALINE DIET FOR DADDY AND SON

2 Books in 1: For Beginners: The Ultimate Guide of Alkaline Herbal Medicine for permanent weight loss, Understand pH with 200+ Anti Inflammatory Recipes Cookbook! Plant-Based Recipes Are Included!

THE ALKALINE DIET FAST & EASY

2 Books in 1: The Complete and Exhaustive Beginner's Guide to lose Weight, Fasting and Revitalize Your Body with Plant-Based Diet including 200+ Healthy and Tasty Recipes!

THE ALKALINE DIET FOR MUM AND KIDDOS

2 Books in 1: The Simplest Alkaline Diet Guide for Beginners + 200 Easy Recipes: How to Cure Your Body, Lose Weight and Regain Your Life with Easy Alkaline Diet Cookbook! Plant-Based Recipes Are Included!

THE ALKALINE DIET TO LOSE WEIGHT FAST

3 Books in 1: The Revolution of Eating Habits to stay Healthy and Find the Best Shape. A complete Program with 300+ Recipes to Regain a Healthy Balance of the Body with Alkaline Foods and lose Weight Quickly.

THE ALKALINE DIET FOR A HEALTHY FAMILY

3 Books in 1: A Complete Guide for Beginners to Clean and Treat Your Body, Eat Well with More Than 300+ Easy Alkaline Recipes for Weight Loss and Fight Chronic Disease!

THE ALKALINE DIET HIGH-PROTEIN FOR SPORT PLAYERS

3 Books in 1: Diet for Beginners: Top 300+ Alkaline Recipes for Weight Loss with Plant Based Diet And 21 Secrets To Reset And Understand pH Right Now!

THE ALKALINE DIET FOR ABSOLUTE BEGINNERS

3 Books in 1: This Cookbook Includes: Alkaline Diet for Beginners + Alkaline Diet Cookbook, The Best Guidebook to Understanding pH Secrets with More Than 300+ Recipes for Weight Loss and Anti-Inflammatory Action!

THE ALKALINE DIET COMPLETE EDITION FOR EVERYBODY

4 Books in 1: The complete guide to eat well and Lose Weight while understanding pH and prevent disease to boost your everyday energy! 400+ Recipes with Plant-Based Recipes Included!

CONCLUSIONS

Congratulations! You made it to the end!

Thank you for making it to the end of the Alkaline Diet; we hope it was informative and provided all you need to reach your goals, whatever they may be.

With the information you have, you can now start a successful alkaline diet. Your body works best when it's not acidic. The alkaline diet ensures that your body functions at its best. The great thing is that all the food you can eat is tasty. With the recipes in this book, you won't have to worry about making dinner. So don't wait any longer. Start today, and you will see your body change for the better.

The purpose of this cookbook was to introduce readers to most of the insights regarding the alkaline diet in a comprehensive way. Therefore, the text of this book has been categorized into several sections, each of which discusses the basics, the details, what it has and what it doesn't, and recipes related to the alkaline diet. In addition, the recipe chapter is divided into subsections, ranging from breakfast to lunch, dinner, smoothies, snacks, and desserts. So take some time to travel the length of this book and experience the miraculous effects of an alkaline diet on your mind and health.

Laura Green

CPSIA information can be obtained
at www.ICGtesting.com
Printed in the USA
BVHW010453220621
610124BV00008B/1474